50 Thailand Breakfast Recipes for Home

By: Kelly Johnson

Table of Contents

- Thai Omelette (Kai Jeow)
- Congee with Pork (Khao Tom Moo)
- Thai Rice Porridge (Jok)
- Thai Sweet Sticky Rice (Khao Niew)
- Thai Roti with Condensed Milk (Roti Gluay)
- Thai Breakfast Soup (Khao Tom)
- Thai Steamed Dumplings (Khanom Jeeb)
- Thai Coconut Pancakes (Khanom Krok)
- Thai Fried Rice (Khao Pad)
- Thai Pandan Pancakes (Khanom Babin)
- Thai Fried Dough Sticks (Patongko)
- Thai Coconut Milk Sticky Rice (Khao Tom Mat)
- Thai Toast with Pandan Custard (Khanom Pang Sang Ka Ya)
- Thai Coconut Pudding (Khanom Tuay)
- Thai Spicy Minced Pork Salad (Laab Moo)
- Thai Stir-Fried Noodles (Pad Thai)
- Thai Fish Congee (Jok Pla)
- Thai Chicken Curry with Rice Noodles (Khao Soi)
- Thai Spicy Pork Salad (Nam Tok Moo)
- Thai Pork Satay (Moo Satay)
- Thai Spicy Green Papaya Salad (Som Tum)
- Thai Stir-Fried Morning Glory (Pad Pak Boong)
- Thai Grilled Chicken (Gai Yang)
- Thai Grilled Pork Skewers (Moo Ping)
- Thai Stir-Fried Rice Noodles (Pad See Ew)
- Thai Red Curry with Rice (Khao Pad Prik Gaeng)
- Thai Sweet Coconut Soup (Tub Tim Grob)
- Thai Stir-Fried Eggplant (Pad Makua Yao)
- Thai Chicken and Rice Soup (Khao Man Gai)
- Thai Mango Sticky Rice (Khao Niew Mamuang)
- Thai Steamed Dumplings with Peanut Sauce (Khanom Jeeb Sai)
- Thai Steamed Fish Custard (Hor Mok)
- Thai Cucumber Relish (Ajat)
- Thai Fried Taro Dumplings (Khanom Phing)
- Thai Coconut Pancakes with Corn (Khanom Khrok Khao Pod)

- Thai Shrimp Congee (Jok Goong)
- Thai Spicy Beef Salad (Yam Nua)
- Thai Stir-Fried Glass Noodles (Pad Woon Sen)
- Thai Pork and Rice Congee (Khao Tom Moo)
- Thai Coconut Milk Custard (Sangkhaya)
- Thai Peanut Pancakes (Khanom Thua Paep)
- Thai Spicy Squid Salad (Yam Pla Muk)
- Thai Stir-Fried Pork with Basil (Pad Kra Pao Moo)
- Thai Coconut Ice Cream (I-Tim Kati)
- Thai Fish Cakes (Tod Mun Pla)
- Thai Deep Fried Bananas (Kluay Tod)
- Thai Chicken Curry with Bamboo Shoots (Gang Kiew Wan Gai)
- Thai Spicy Noodle Soup (Tom Yum Goong)
- Thai Fried Rice with Shrimp (Khao Pad Goong)
- Thai Grilled Pork Neck Salad (Yam Kor Moo Yang)

Thai Omelette (Kai Jeow)

Ingredients:

- 2-3 eggs
- 1-2 tablespoons fish sauce
- 1 tablespoon soy sauce (optional)
- Vegetable oil, for frying
- Freshly ground black pepper
- Thai jasmine rice, to serve (optional)

Instructions:

1. **Beat the Eggs:**
    - Crack the eggs into a mixing bowl. Add fish sauce and soy sauce (if using). Beat the mixture well until the yolks and whites are fully combined and slightly frothy.
2. **Heat the Pan:**
    - Place a non-stick frying pan over medium-high heat. Add enough vegetable oil to coat the bottom of the pan.
3. **Fry the Omelette:**
    - Once the oil is hot (but not smoking), pour the beaten egg mixture into the pan. The mixture should sizzle as it hits the pan.
    - Tilt the pan to spread the egg evenly into a round shape. Let it cook undisturbed for about 1-2 minutes, or until the bottom is golden brown and set.
4. **Flip and Cook:**
    - Carefully flip the omelette using a spatula. Cook the other side for another 1-2 minutes, or until it's cooked through and golden brown.
5. **Serve:**
    - Slide the omelette onto a plate. Sprinkle freshly ground black pepper over the top, if desired.
    - Serve hot with Thai jasmine rice, and perhaps some sliced cucumbers or a side of Sriracha sauce for extra flavor.

Tips:

- You can customize your Thai omelette by adding minced pork, onions, tomatoes, or other ingredients to the beaten eggs before frying.
- Thai omelettes are often served with a dipping sauce made from fish sauce, lime juice, and chopped chilies.
- Adjust the amount of fish sauce and soy sauce according to your taste preference.

Enjoy your delicious Thai omelette (Kai Jeow)!

Congee with Pork (Khao Tom Moo)

Ingredients:

- 1 cup jasmine rice
- 6 cups water or chicken broth
- 250g ground pork
- 2-3 cloves garlic, minced
- 1 tablespoon grated ginger
- 2 tablespoons fish sauce
- White pepper, to taste
- Green onions, thinly sliced, for garnish
- Fresh cilantro leaves, chopped, for garnish
- Fried garlic, for garnish (optional)
- Hard-boiled eggs, halved, for serving (optional)

Instructions:

1. **Prepare the Rice:**
   - Rinse the jasmine rice under cold water until the water runs clear. This helps remove excess starch.
2. **Cook the Congee:**
   - In a large pot, bring the water or chicken broth to a boil over medium-high heat.
   - Add the rinsed rice to the boiling water. Stir occasionally to prevent sticking.
   - Reduce the heat to low and let the rice simmer, uncovered, stirring occasionally, for about 30-40 minutes or until the rice grains are fully softened and the mixture has thickened to a porridge-like consistency.
3. **Prepare the Pork Mixture:**
   - While the congee is cooking, in a separate pan, heat a bit of oil over medium heat.
   - Add minced garlic and grated ginger. Sauté for about 1 minute until fragrant.
   - Add the ground pork to the pan, breaking it up with a spoon. Cook until the pork is browned and cooked through.
   - Season with fish sauce and white pepper to taste. Mix well.
4. **Combine and Serve:**
   - Once the congee is thick and creamy, add the cooked pork mixture into the pot of congee. Stir well to combine.
   - Taste and adjust seasoning if needed with more fish sauce or white pepper.
5. **Garnish and Serve:**
   - Ladle the hot congee into bowls. Garnish with sliced green onions, chopped cilantro, and fried garlic (if using).
   - Serve hot with optional hard-boiled eggs on the side.

Tips:

- You can customize your Khao Tom Moo by adding toppings like crispy fried shallots, chopped peanuts, or a drizzle of sesame oil for extra flavor.
- Leftover congee can be stored in the refrigerator for a few days. Reheat gently on the stove, adding a bit of water or broth to adjust the consistency.

Enjoy your comforting bowl of Thai Congee with Pork (Khao Tom Moo)! It's perfect for warming up on chilly mornings or as a soothing meal anytime.

Thai Rice Porridge (Jok)

Ingredients:

- 1 cup jasmine rice
- 8 cups chicken broth (or water)
- 250g ground pork or chicken
- 2-3 cloves garlic, minced
- 1 tablespoon grated ginger
- 2 tablespoons fish sauce
- 1 tablespoon soy sauce
- White pepper, to taste
- Green onions, thinly sliced, for garnish
- Fresh cilantro leaves, chopped, for garnish
- Fried garlic, for garnish (optional)
- Preserved or salted duck eggs, sliced, for serving (optional)

Instructions:

1. **Prepare the Rice:**
   - Rinse the jasmine rice under cold water until the water runs clear. This helps remove excess starch.
2. **Cook the Porridge:**
   - In a large pot, bring the chicken broth (or water) to a boil over medium-high heat.
   - Add the rinsed rice to the boiling broth. Stir well to combine.
   - Reduce the heat to low and let the rice simmer, uncovered, stirring occasionally to prevent sticking. Cook for about 30-40 minutes or until the rice grains are fully softened and the mixture has thickened to a porridge-like consistency.
3. **Prepare the Pork Mixture:**
   - While the porridge is cooking, in a separate pan, heat a bit of oil over medium heat.
   - Add minced garlic and grated ginger. Sauté for about 1 minute until fragrant.
   - Add the ground pork (or chicken) to the pan, breaking it up with a spoon. Cook until the meat is browned and cooked through.
   - Season with fish sauce, soy sauce, and white pepper to taste. Mix well.
4. **Combine and Serve:**
   - Once the porridge is thick and creamy, add the cooked pork mixture into the pot of porridge. Stir well to combine.
   - Taste and adjust seasoning if needed with more fish sauce, soy sauce, or white pepper.
5. **Garnish and Serve:**
   - Ladle the hot Jok into bowls. Garnish with sliced green onions, chopped cilantro, and fried garlic (if using).
   - Serve hot with optional sliced preserved or salted duck eggs on the side.

Tips:

- Jok is typically served with condiments such as sliced ginger, chopped green onions, cilantro, fried garlic, and a dash of white pepper. Feel free to adjust the toppings according to your preference.
- Leftover Jok can be stored in the refrigerator for a few days. Reheat gently on the stove, adding a bit of water or broth to adjust the consistency.

Enjoy your comforting bowl of Thai Rice Porridge (Jok)! It's a delicious way to start your day or to enjoy as a light meal any time.

Thai Sweet Sticky Rice (Khao Niew)

Ingredients:

- 2 cups glutinous rice (also known as sticky rice)
- 1 can (400ml) coconut milk
- 1/2 cup sugar (adjust to taste)
- 1/2 teaspoon salt
- Mangoes, peeled and sliced (optional, for serving)

Instructions:

1. **Soak the Sticky Rice:**
   - Rinse the glutinous rice under cold water until the water runs clear. Then, soak the rice in water for at least 4 hours or overnight. This step is crucial to soften the rice and ensure it cooks evenly.
2. **Steam the Sticky Rice:**
   - Drain the soaked rice. Place the rice in a steamer lined with cheesecloth or a muslin cloth. Steam over medium heat for about 25-30 minutes, or until the rice is tender and cooked through.
3. **Prepare the Coconut Sauce:**
   - While the rice is steaming, prepare the coconut sauce. In a saucepan, combine the coconut milk, sugar, and salt over medium heat. Stir until the sugar dissolves and the mixture is heated through. Do not boil.
4. **Combine and Mix:**
   - Once the sticky rice is cooked, transfer it to a large bowl. Pour half of the warm coconut sauce over the rice. Use a spatula or wooden spoon to gently fold and mix the sauce into the rice. Allow the rice to absorb the sauce for about 10 minutes.
5. **Serve:**
   - Serve the sweet sticky rice warm or at room temperature. Drizzle the remaining coconut sauce over the top. Optionally, serve with fresh mango slices on the side.

Tips:

- Glutinous rice is essential for this dish as it has a sticky texture when cooked, unlike regular rice varieties.
- Adjust the sweetness of the coconut sauce according to your taste. You can add more or less sugar depending on how sweet you prefer the dessert.
- If you don't have a steamer, you can cook the soaked glutinous rice in a rice cooker using the steaming function.

Thai Sweet Sticky Rice (Khao Niew) with Coconut Sauce is a delightful treat that showcases the richness of coconut milk and the unique texture of glutinous rice. It's perfect for breakfast or as a sweet ending to any meal. Enjoy!

Thai Roti with Condensed Milk (Roti Gluay)

Ingredients:

- 1 cup all-purpose flour
- 1/4 teaspoon salt
- 1 tablespoon sugar
- 1/2 cup water
- Vegetable oil, for frying
- 1-2 ripe bananas, thinly sliced
- Sweetened condensed milk, for drizzling

Instructions:

1. **Prepare the Dough:**
   - In a mixing bowl, combine the all-purpose flour, salt, and sugar. Gradually add the water while mixing until a dough forms. Knead the dough on a lightly floured surface until smooth and elastic. Cover the dough and let it rest for about 15-20 minutes.
2. **Shape the Roti:**
   - Divide the rested dough into 4 equal portions. Roll each portion into a ball. On a lightly floured surface, roll out each ball of dough into a thin circle or oval shape, about 6-8 inches in diameter.
3. **Fry the Roti:**
   - Heat a bit of vegetable oil in a non-stick frying pan over medium heat. Carefully place one rolled-out dough into the pan. Fry for about 1-2 minutes on each side, or until golden brown and crispy. Repeat with the remaining dough portions, adding more oil to the pan as needed.
4. **Assemble the Roti Gluay:**
   - Once all the rotis are fried, place them on a serving plate. Top each roti with thinly sliced bananas.
5. **Serve:**
   - Drizzle sweetened condensed milk generously over the bananas and the roti. Serve immediately while warm.

Tips:

- You can customize Roti Gluay by adding other toppings such as chocolate syrup, Nutella, or crushed peanuts.
- Adjust the sweetness by adding more or less condensed milk according to your preference.
- Roti Gluay is best enjoyed fresh and warm, straight from the pan.

Enjoy your homemade Thai Roti with Condensed Milk (Roti Gluay)! It's a delightful treat that combines crispy fried dough with sweet bananas and creamy condensed milk.

Thai Breakfast Soup (Khao Tom)

Ingredients:

- 4 cups water or chicken broth
- 1 cup jasmine rice, rinsed
- 250g ground pork or chicken
- 2-3 cloves garlic, minced
- 1-2 shallots, finely chopped
- 1-inch piece of ginger, thinly sliced
- 2-3 green onions, thinly sliced
- Fish sauce, to taste
- Soy sauce, to taste
- White pepper, to taste
- Salt, to taste
- Fresh cilantro leaves, chopped (for garnish)
- Fried garlic (optional, for garnish)
- Fried shallots (optional, for garnish)

Instructions:

1. **Prepare the Rice**: In a large pot, bring the water or chicken broth to a boil. Add the rinsed jasmine rice and reduce heat to a simmer. Cook until the rice is soft and has broken down slightly, stirring occasionally to prevent sticking (about 20-30 minutes).
2. **Cook the Pork or Chicken**: While the rice is cooking, heat a separate pan over medium heat. Add a little oil if needed, then add the minced garlic, chopped shallots, and sliced ginger. Sauté until fragrant.
3. **Add Ground Meat**: Add the ground pork or chicken to the pan with the aromatics. Break it up with a spoon and cook until browned and cooked through.
4. **Combine Everything**: Once the rice is cooked and slightly broken down, add the cooked pork or chicken mixture into the pot with the rice and broth. Stir to combine well.
5. **Season**: Season the soup with fish sauce, soy sauce, white pepper, and salt to taste. Adjust the seasoning according to your preference.
6. **Serve**: Ladle the Khao Tom into bowls. Garnish each bowl with sliced green onions, chopped cilantro, fried garlic, and/or fried shallots.
7. **Enjoy**: Serve hot and enjoy this delicious and comforting Thai breakfast soup!

Variations:

- **Seafood Khao Tom**: Substitute the ground meat with seafood such as shrimp or fish fillets.
- **Vegetarian Khao Tom**: Use vegetable broth and add tofu or mushrooms instead of meat.

- **Egg Khao Tom**: Crack an egg into the hot soup and stir gently for an added protein boost.

Khao Tom is versatile and can be adjusted to suit your taste preferences. It's hearty enough for breakfast but can also be enjoyed any time of the day.

Thai Steamed Dumplings (Khanom Jeeb)

Ingredients:

For the Filling:

- 150g ground pork
- 150g shrimp, peeled, deveined, and finely chopped
- 2-3 cloves garlic, minced
- 2-3 water chestnuts, finely chopped (optional, for crunch)
- 1 tablespoon soy sauce
- 1 tablespoon oyster sauce
- 1 teaspoon sugar
- 1/2 teaspoon white pepper
- 1/2 teaspoon sesame oil
- 1 tablespoon cornstarch
- Chopped cilantro leaves (optional)

For the Dumpling Wrappers:

- Round dumpling wrappers (store-bought or homemade)

For Serving:

- Soy sauce, for dipping
- Fresh cilantro leaves, chopped (optional)
- Fried garlic (optional)
- Sliced red chili (optional)

Instructions:

1. **Prepare the Filling**:
   - In a mixing bowl, combine the ground pork, chopped shrimp, minced garlic, water chestnuts (if using), soy sauce, oyster sauce, sugar, white pepper, sesame oil, cornstarch, and chopped cilantro (if using). Mix well until all ingredients are evenly incorporated.
2. **Assemble the Dumplings**:
   - Take a dumpling wrapper and place a small spoonful of the filling mixture in the center (about 1 teaspoon). Fold the wrapper in half over the filling to create a half-moon shape. Pinch and pleat the edges together to seal. Repeat until all the filling or wrappers are used up.
3. **Steam the Dumplings**:
   - Line a steamer basket with parchment paper or cabbage leaves to prevent sticking. Arrange the dumplings in the steamer basket, leaving some space between each dumpling to prevent them from sticking together during steaming.

- Steam the dumplings over boiling water for about 8-10 minutes, or until the filling is cooked through and the dumpling wrappers are translucent and tender.
4. **Serve**:
    - Carefully remove the steamed dumplings from the steamer and arrange them on a serving plate.
    - Serve hot with soy sauce for dipping. Garnish with chopped cilantro leaves, fried garlic, and sliced red chili if desired.
5. **Enjoy**:
    - Khanom Jeeb is best enjoyed fresh and hot. Serve as an appetizer or snack and savor the delicious flavors of these Thai steamed dumplings!

Tips:

- Make sure the dumpling wrappers are sealed tightly to prevent the filling from leaking out during steaming.
- You can make a large batch of Khanom Jeeb and freeze them before steaming for later use. Just ensure they are properly sealed to prevent freezer burn.
- Adjust the seasoning of the filling according to your taste preferences. You can add more soy sauce, sugar, or white pepper as needed.

These Thai steamed dumplings are a wonderful treat that showcases the delicate flavors of pork and shrimp, complemented by aromatic garlic and soy sauce. Enjoy making and sharing Khanom Jeeb with friends and family!

Thai Coconut Pancakes (Khanom Krok)

Ingredients:

Batter:

- 1 cup rice flour
- 1/2 cup all-purpose flour
- 1 cup coconut milk
- 1 cup water
- 1/2 cup sugar
- 1/4 teaspoon salt

Topping (optional):

- Sweet corn kernels
- Scallions, chopped
- Cooked taro, diced
- Cooked pumpkin, diced
- Cooked mung beans

For Cooking:

- Coconut oil or vegetable oil for greasing the pan

Instructions:

1. **Prepare the Batter**:
   - In a mixing bowl, combine the rice flour, all-purpose flour, coconut milk, water, sugar, and salt. Whisk until smooth and well combined. The batter should have a thin consistency, similar to pancake batter.
2. **Heat the Pan**:
   - Preheat a Khanom Krok pan or a small round pancake pan over medium heat. If you don't have a specific Khanom Krok pan, you can use a small round-bottomed pan.
3. **Grease the Pan**:
   - Lightly grease each indentation of the pan with coconut oil or vegetable oil using a brush or paper towel.
4. **Pour the Batter**:
   - Once the pan is hot, pour a small amount of batter into each indentation, filling them about 3/4 full.
5. **Add Toppings (Optional)**:
   - If desired, add a few pieces of sweet corn kernels, chopped scallions, diced cooked taro, cooked pumpkin, or cooked mung beans on top of each pancake.
6. **Cover and Cook**:

- Cover the pan with a lid and cook the pancakes for about 4-5 minutes, or until the edges are golden brown and crispy, and the tops are set.
7. **Flip (Optional)**:
   - If you prefer, you can flip the pancakes halfway through cooking to ensure both sides are evenly cooked. Use a spoon or chopsticks to carefully flip them.
8. **Serve**:
   - Once cooked through and golden brown, remove the Khanom Krok from the pan and transfer them to a serving plate. They should be crispy on the outside and soft and custardy on the inside.
9. **Enjoy**:
   - Serve Khanom Krok warm as a snack or dessert. They can be enjoyed on their own or with a cup of Thai tea or coffee.

Tips:

- Khanom Krok pans are traditionally made of cast iron or aluminum with multiple small round indentations. If you don't have a Khanom Krok pan, you can use a small takoyaki pan or any similar pan with round indentations.
- Adjust the amount of sugar according to your preference. You can also use palm sugar for a more traditional flavor.
- Experiment with different toppings to create variations of Khanom Krok. Traditional toppings include sweet corn and scallions, but you can get creative with fruits or other ingredients.

Making Khanom Krok at home allows you to enjoy this delicious Thai street food anytime. The combination of coconut milk and rice flour gives these pancakes a unique texture and flavor that's both crispy and creamy.

Thai Fried Rice (Khao Pad)

Ingredients:

- 3 cups cooked jasmine rice (preferably leftover and cooled)
- 2 tablespoons vegetable oil
- 2 cloves garlic, minced
- 1 shallot, finely chopped
- 1-2 Thai chilies, finely chopped (optional, adjust to taste)
- 150g chicken, pork, shrimp, or tofu, diced (optional)
- 1 egg, lightly beaten
- 1/2 cup mixed vegetables (e.g., peas, carrots, bell peppers)
- 2 tablespoons soy sauce
- 1 tablespoon fish sauce
- 1 teaspoon sugar
- 1/4 teaspoon white pepper
- Green onions, chopped, for garnish
- Fresh cilantro leaves, chopped, for garnish
- Lime wedges, for serving

Instructions:

1. **Prepare Ingredients**:
   - If you haven't already, cook the jasmine rice and let it cool. It's best to use leftover rice as it fries better.
2. **Heat Oil**:
   - Heat vegetable oil in a wok or large frying pan over medium-high heat.
3. **Stir-Fry Aromatics**:
   - Add minced garlic, chopped shallot, and Thai chilies (if using) to the hot oil. Stir-fry for about 30 seconds until fragrant.
4. **Add Protein (if using)**:
   - Push the garlic and shallot mixture to the side of the wok/pan and add diced chicken, pork, shrimp, or tofu. Stir-fry until the protein is cooked through.
5. **Cook Egg**:
   - Push the protein to the side and pour the lightly beaten egg into the empty space. Let it cook for a few seconds until it starts to set, then scramble it with a spatula until cooked through.
6. **Add Vegetables**:
   - Add mixed vegetables to the wok/pan and stir-fry for 1-2 minutes until they are cooked but still crisp.
7. **Add Rice**:
   - Add the cooked jasmine rice to the wok/pan. Use a spatula to break up any clumps and stir-fry everything together for a few minutes.
8. **Season**:

- Drizzle soy sauce, fish sauce, sugar, and white pepper over the rice mixture. Stir well to combine and evenly distribute the seasonings. Taste and adjust seasoning if needed.
9. **Finish and Serve**:
    - Remove the wok/pan from the heat. Stir in chopped green onions and fresh cilantro leaves.
10. **Garnish and Serve**:
    - Transfer the Khao Pad to serving plates or bowls. Garnish with additional chopped green onions and cilantro if desired. Serve hot with lime wedges on the side.

Tips:

- **Use cold, leftover rice**: It fries up better and is less likely to become mushy compared to freshly cooked rice.
- **Customize with proteins**: Feel free to use chicken, pork, shrimp, tofu, or a combination. Ensure they are cooked through before proceeding with the recipe.
- **Adjust heat level**: Control the spiciness by adjusting the amount of Thai chilies used or omitting them altogether.
- **Add more vegetables**: You can add more vegetables such as broccoli, mushrooms, or baby corn for extra flavor and texture.

Khao Pad is a versatile dish that can be adapted to suit your taste preferences and ingredient availability. It's perfect for a quick and satisfying meal any time of the day!

Thai Pandan Pancakes (Khanom Babin)

Ingredients:

For the Batter:

- 1 cup rice flour
- 1/2 cup all-purpose flour
- 1/2 cup sugar
- 1/4 teaspoon salt
- 1 cup coconut milk
- 1/2 cup water
- 1 tablespoon pandan juice (or pandan extract)
- 1/4 teaspoon baking powder

For the Filling:

- 1 cup grated coconut (fresh or frozen)
- 1/2 cup palm sugar (or brown sugar)
- 1/4 cup water
- A pinch of salt

For Cooking:

- Vegetable oil or coconut oil for greasing the pan

Instructions:

1. **Prepare the Filling**:
   - In a small saucepan, combine the grated coconut, palm sugar, water, and a pinch of salt. Cook over medium heat, stirring continuously, until the sugar has dissolved and the mixture becomes sticky and slightly caramelized. Remove from heat and let it cool.
2. **Make the Batter**:
   - In a mixing bowl, whisk together the rice flour, all-purpose flour, sugar, and salt.
   - Gradually add the coconut milk, water, pandan juice (or extract), and baking powder to the dry ingredients. Whisk until smooth and well combined. The batter should have a thin consistency similar to pancake batter.
3. **Heat the Pan**:
   - Heat a non-stick frying pan or a Khanom Babin pan (if available) over medium heat. Lightly grease the pan with vegetable oil or coconut oil using a brush or paper towel.
4. **Cook the Pancakes**:
   - Pour a small amount of batter into the pan, just enough to cover the bottom in a thin layer (similar to making crepes). Swirl the pan to spread the batter evenly.

5. **Add the Filling**:
   - Spoon a small amount of the coconut-palm sugar filling onto one half of the pancake. Fold the other half of the pancake over the filling to create a half-moon shape.
6. **Cook Until Golden Brown**:
   - Cook the filled pancakes for about 2-3 minutes on each side, or until they are golden brown and crispy.
7. **Repeat**:
   - Repeat the process with the remaining batter and filling until all pancakes are cooked.
8. **Serve**:
   - Serve Khanom Babin warm or at room temperature. They can be enjoyed on their own as a snack or dessert.

Tips:

- **Pandan Juice**: To make pandan juice, blend fresh or thawed frozen pandan leaves with a little water until finely chopped, then strain through a fine sieve to extract the juice.
- **Adjust Filling**: Feel free to adjust the sweetness of the filling by adding more or less palm sugar according to your taste.
- **Storage**: Khanom Babin are best enjoyed fresh, but they can be stored in an airtight container at room temperature for a day or two. Reheat briefly in a pan or microwave before serving if desired.

Khanom Babin showcases the unique flavors of pandan and coconut, creating a delicious and aromatic treat that's popular in Thai cuisine. Enjoy making and savoring these delightful pancakes!

Thai Fried Dough Sticks (Patongko)

Ingredients:

- 2 cups all-purpose flour
- 1 tablespoon baking powder
- 1/2 teaspoon salt
- 1 tablespoon sugar
- 1 cup warm water
- Vegetable oil for frying

Instructions:

1. **Prepare the Dough**:
    - In a mixing bowl, combine the all-purpose flour, baking powder, salt, and sugar. Mix well.
    - Gradually add the warm water to the dry ingredients, stirring with a spoon or spatula until a dough starts to form.
2. **Knead the Dough**:
    - Transfer the dough to a clean surface and knead it for about 5-7 minutes until it becomes smooth and elastic. If the dough is too sticky, you can dust a little more flour as needed.
3. **Rest the Dough**:
    - Place the dough back into the mixing bowl and cover it with a damp cloth or plastic wrap. Let it rest at room temperature for about 30 minutes.
4. **Shape the Dough**:
    - After resting, divide the dough into 2 equal portions. Take one portion and roll it out into a rectangle about 1/2 inch thick.
5. **Cut into Strips**:
    - Use a sharp knife or pizza cutter to cut the dough into strips about 1 inch wide and 6-8 inches long. You can adjust the size according to your preference.
6. **Shape the Sticks**:
    - Take each strip of dough and stretch it gently to elongate it slightly. Fold each strip in half lengthwise, press lightly to seal, and set aside. Repeat with the remaining strips.
7. **Fry the Dough Sticks**:
    - Heat vegetable oil in a deep frying pan or wok over medium-high heat until it reaches about 350-360°F (175-180°C).
    - Carefully lower a few dough sticks into the hot oil. Fry them in batches, turning occasionally, until they are golden brown and crispy on all sides, about 3-4 minutes per batch.
8. **Drain and Serve**:
    - Remove the fried dough sticks with a slotted spoon or tongs and drain them on paper towels to remove excess oil.

9. **Serve Warm**:
   - Serve Patongko warm with sweetened condensed milk, pandan custard, Thai tea, or any dipping sauce of your choice.

Tips:

- **Oil Temperature**: Maintain a consistent oil temperature while frying to ensure the dough sticks cook evenly and become crispy.
- **Storage**: Patongko are best enjoyed fresh and hot. However, you can store any leftovers in an airtight container at room temperature for up to a day. Reheat them briefly in the oven or toaster oven before serving.
- **Variations**: Some recipes add a touch of sesame seeds or black sesame seeds to the dough for extra flavor and texture.

Patongko are deliciously crispy on the outside and soft and fluffy on the inside, making them a favorite among Thai street foods. Enjoy making and indulging in these delightful fried dough sticks at home!

Patongko (Thai Fried Dough Sticks)

Ingredients:

- 2 cups all-purpose flour
- 1 tablespoon baking powder
- 1/2 teaspoon salt
- 1 tablespoon sugar
- 1 cup warm water
- Vegetable oil for frying

Instructions:

1. **Prepare the Dough:**
    - In a mixing bowl, combine flour, baking powder, salt, and sugar. Mix well.
    - Gradually add warm water to the dry ingredients, stirring until a dough forms.
2. **Knead the Dough:**
    - Transfer dough to a clean surface and knead for 5-7 minutes until smooth and elastic. Add more flour if sticky.
3. **Rest the Dough:**
    - Place dough back in the bowl, cover with a damp cloth or plastic wrap, and let rest for 30 minutes at room temperature.
4. **Shape the Dough:**
    - Divide dough into 2 portions. Roll out each portion into a 1/2 inch thick rectangle.
    - Cut into strips about 1 inch wide and 6-8 inches long. Fold each strip in half lengthwise and press lightly to seal.
5. **Fry the Dough Sticks:**
    - Heat vegetable oil in a pan to 350-360°F (175-180°C).
    - Fry dough sticks in batches until golden brown and crispy, about 3-4 minutes per batch. Turn occasionally.
6. **Drain and Serve:**
    - Remove fried dough sticks with a slotted spoon or tongs. Drain on paper towels to remove excess oil.
7. **Serve Warm:**
    - Serve Patongko warm with sweetened condensed milk, pandan custard, Thai tea, or your favorite dipping sauce.

Tips:

- **Oil Temperature:** Maintain consistent oil temperature for even cooking.
- **Storage:** Best enjoyed fresh; store leftovers in an airtight container at room temperature and reheat briefly before serving.
- **Variations:** Consider adding sesame seeds for extra flavor and texture.

Enjoy your homemade Patongko, crispy on the outside and fluffy on the inside—a delightful Thai street food experience at home!

Thai Coconut Milk Sticky Rice (Khao Tom Mat)

Ingredients:

For the Sticky Rice:

- 1 cup glutinous rice (sticky rice)
- 1 cup coconut milk
- 1/2 cup sugar
- 1/2 teaspoon salt

For Wrapping:

- Banana leaves, cut into squares (about 6-8 inches)

Instructions:

1. **Prepare the Sticky Rice:**
    - Rinse the glutinous rice in cold water until the water runs clear. Soak the rice in water for at least 2 hours or overnight.
2. **Cook the Sticky Rice:**
    - Drain the soaked rice and steam it in a bamboo steamer or a regular steamer lined with cheesecloth or a clean cloth, for about 20-25 minutes, or until the rice is tender and cooked through.
3. **Prepare the Coconut Milk Mixture:**
    - In a small saucepan, heat the coconut milk over medium heat. Add sugar and salt, stirring until dissolved. Simmer for 5 minutes until slightly thickened. Remove from heat.
4. **Mix Coconut Milk with Sticky Rice:**
    - Transfer the steamed sticky rice to a mixing bowl. Gradually pour the coconut milk mixture over the rice, stirring gently to coat the rice evenly. Let the rice absorb the coconut milk mixture for about 10-15 minutes.
5. **Wrap the Khao Tom Mat:**
    - Take a piece of banana leaf and place a small portion of the sticky rice mixture in the center (about 2 tablespoons). Fold the banana leaf over the rice to form a rectangular packet. Secure the edges with a toothpick or fold tightly.
6. **Steam the Wrapped Rice:**
    - Arrange the wrapped rice packets in a steamer basket. Steam over medium-high heat for about 15-20 minutes, or until the rice is fully cooked and has absorbed the flavors of the banana leaf.
7. **Serve:**
    - Remove the Khao Tom Mat from the steamer and let them cool slightly before serving. Serve warm or at room temperature.

Tips:

- **Banana Leaves:** If using fresh banana leaves, briefly pass them over a flame or steam them to make them pliable before wrapping the rice.
- **Variations:** You can add toppings such as sesame seeds or roasted mung beans to the sticky rice mixture for added texture and flavor.
- **Storage:** Khao Tom Mat can be stored in an airtight container in the refrigerator for up to 2 days. Reheat gently in a steamer before serving.

Khao Tom Mat is a delightful Thai dessert with a wonderful blend of sweet coconut milk and sticky rice, wrapped in aromatic banana leaves. Enjoy making and sharing this traditional treat!

Thai Toast with Pandan Custard (Khanom Pang Sang Ka Ya)

Ingredients:

For the Pandan Custard:

- 1/2 cup coconut milk
- 1/2 cup fresh pandan juice (blend fresh or thawed frozen pandan leaves with water and strain)
- 3 egg yolks
- 1/2 cup sugar
- 1 tablespoon cornstarch
- A pinch of salt

For the Toast:

- Slices of bread (white or whole wheat)
- Butter or margarine, softened

For Garnish (optional):

- Toasted shredded coconut
- Fresh pandan leaves for decoration

Instructions:

1. **Prepare the Pandan Custard:**
   - In a saucepan, combine the coconut milk and pandan juice. Heat over medium heat until it just starts to simmer. Remove from heat and set aside.
   - In a mixing bowl, whisk together the egg yolks, sugar, cornstarch, and salt until well combined and slightly thickened.
   - Gradually pour the warm coconut milk mixture into the egg yolk mixture, whisking constantly to prevent curdling.
   - Pour the mixture back into the saucepan and return to medium heat. Cook, stirring constantly, until the custard thickens to a pudding-like consistency. Remove from heat and let it cool completely.
2. **Prepare the Toast:**
   - Toast slices of bread until golden brown and crispy. Spread butter or margarine on each slice while still warm.
3. **Assemble Khanom Pang Sang Ka Ya:**
   - Spread a generous amount of pandan custard onto each slice of toasted bread.
4. **Garnish (optional):**
   - Sprinkle toasted shredded coconut over the pandan custard for added texture and flavor.
5. **Serve:**

- Arrange the Khanom Pang Sang Ka Ya on a serving platter. Optionally, decorate with fresh pandan leaves for a traditional touch.

Tips:

- **Pandan Juice:** If fresh pandan leaves are not available, you can use pandan extract or pandan paste diluted with water. Adjust the amount according to the desired level of pandan flavor.
- **Storage:** Store any leftover pandan custard in an airtight container in the refrigerator for up to 3 days. Reheat gently before using again.
- **Variations:** You can also serve the pandan custard chilled as a pudding or dessert on its own, or use it as a filling for other pastries or cakes.

Khanom Pang Sang Ka Ya is a delightful Thai dessert that beautifully blends the aromatic flavor of pandan with creamy custard on crispy toast—a perfect treat to enjoy with friends and family!

Thai Coconut Pudding (Khanom Tuay)

Ingredients:

For the Coconut Milk Layer:

- 1 cup coconut milk
- 1/2 cup water
- 3 tablespoons rice flour
- 2 tablespoons sugar
- A pinch of salt

For the Pandan Custard Layer:

- 1 cup coconut milk
- 1/2 cup water
- 3 tablespoons rice flour
- 2 tablespoons sugar
- 1/4 teaspoon pandan extract (adjust to taste)

Instructions:

1. **Prepare the Coconut Milk Layer:**
    - In a saucepan, combine 1 cup coconut milk, 1/2 cup water, 3 tablespoons rice flour, 2 tablespoons sugar, and a pinch of salt.
    - Whisk the mixture until the rice flour and sugar are dissolved and the mixture is smooth.
    - Place the saucepan over medium heat and stir continuously until the mixture thickens. This usually takes about 5-7 minutes.
    - Once thickened, remove from heat and immediately pour the coconut milk mixture into serving cups or molds, filling them about halfway. Set aside to cool and slightly set while preparing the pandan custard layer.
2. **Prepare the Pandan Custard Layer:**
    - In another saucepan, combine 1 cup coconut milk, 1/2 cup water, 3 tablespoons rice flour, 2 tablespoons sugar, and pandan extract.
    - Whisk until well combined and smooth.
    - Place the saucepan over medium heat and stir continuously until the mixture thickens and starts to bubble, similar to the coconut milk layer. This takes about 5-7 minutes.
    - Remove from heat once thickened. Carefully pour the pandan custard mixture over the set coconut milk layer in the serving cups or molds, filling them almost to the top.
3. **Chill and Serve:**
    - Allow the Khanom Tuay to cool to room temperature, then refrigerate for at least 1-2 hours until fully set and chilled.

4. **Serve:**
   - To serve, gently unmold the Khanom Tuay onto serving plates or enjoy them directly from the cups. They can be served chilled or at room temperature.

Tips:

- **Consistency:** Ensure both layers are thick enough to set but still pourable. Adjust the amount of rice flour if needed to achieve the desired consistency.
- **Pandan Flavor:** Pandan extract adds a lovely green color and a unique flavor to the custard layer. Adjust the amount to your preference for color and taste.
- **Storage:** Store leftover Khanom Tuay in the refrigerator in an airtight container. They should keep well for 2-3 days.

Khanom Tuay is a delightful Thai dessert that beautifully blends creamy coconut milk with fragrant pandan custard. It's perfect for any occasion and provides a taste of authentic Thai sweets. Enjoy making and savoring this traditional dessert!

Thai Spicy Minced Pork Salad (Laab Moo)

Ingredients:

- 300g ground pork
- 2 tablespoons rice flour or toasted rice powder
- 3-4 shallots, thinly sliced
- 2-3 spring onions, thinly sliced
- 1-2 fresh Thai chilies, finely chopped (adjust to taste)
- 2 tablespoons fish sauce
- 3 tablespoons lime juice (about 2 limes)
- 1 tablespoon roasted chili flakes (optional)
- 1 teaspoon sugar
- Fresh cilantro leaves, chopped, for garnish
- Fresh mint leaves, chopped, for garnish
- Fresh lettuce leaves, for serving
- Sticky rice, for serving (optional)

Instructions:

1. **Prepare the Ground Pork:**
   - Heat a large non-stick pan over medium heat. Add the ground pork and cook, breaking it up with a spoon, until it is fully cooked and slightly browned. Drain any excess fat if necessary.
2. **Prepare the Rice Flour or Toasted Rice Powder:**
   - If using rice flour, toast it in a dry pan over medium heat until golden brown and fragrant. Grind it into a fine powder using a mortar and pestle or a spice grinder.
   - If using toasted rice powder, grind toasted sticky rice in a mortar and pestle or a spice grinder until finely ground.
3. **Mix the Salad:**
   - In a large mixing bowl, combine the cooked ground pork with the rice flour or toasted rice powder.
   - Add shallots, spring onions, chopped Thai chilies, fish sauce, lime juice, roasted chili flakes (if using), and sugar. Mix well until all ingredients are evenly combined.
4. **Adjust Seasonings:**
   - Taste and adjust the salad to your liking. You can add more fish sauce for saltiness, lime juice for acidity, or sugar to balance the flavors. Adjust the amount of chili flakes or fresh chilies for spiciness.
5. **Serve:**
   - Transfer the Laab Moo to a serving plate or bowl. Garnish with chopped cilantro and mint leaves.
6. **To Eat:**

- Serve Laab Moo with fresh lettuce leaves and sticky rice on the side. To eat, take a lettuce leaf, scoop some Laab Moo onto it, and enjoy the combination of flavors and textures.

Tips:

- **Toasted Rice Powder:** Toasted sticky rice adds a nutty flavor and helps absorb the juices in the salad. It's a traditional element in Laab Moo.
- **Spice Level:** Adjust the amount of Thai chilies or roasted chili flakes according to your preference for spiciness.
- **Variations:** You can substitute ground pork with ground chicken, beef, or even tofu for different variations of Laab.
- **Storage:** Laab Moo is best enjoyed fresh but can be stored in an airtight container in the refrigerator for up to 2 days. The flavors may intensify as it sits.

Laab Moo is a refreshing and flavorful Thai salad that's packed with herbs and spices. It's a great dish to serve as part of a Thai meal or as a main dish for lunch or dinner. Enjoy making and sharing this authentic Thai recipe!

Thai Stir-Fried Noodles (Pad Thai)

Ingredients:

- 200g rice noodles (dried, about 1/4 inch wide)
- 200g shrimp, peeled and deveined (you can also use chicken, tofu, or keep it vegetarian)
- 2 tablespoons vegetable oil
- 3 cloves garlic, minced
- 1 shallot, finely chopped
- 1/4 cup dried shrimp (optional, but adds traditional flavor)
- 2 eggs, lightly beaten
- 1 cup bean sprouts
- 3-4 spring onions, cut into 2-inch pieces
- 1/4 cup roasted peanuts, finely chopped
- Lime wedges, for serving

For the Pad Thai Sauce:

- 3 tablespoons tamarind paste
- 3 tablespoons fish sauce
- 2 tablespoons palm sugar (or brown sugar)
- 1 tablespoon soy sauce
- 1/2 teaspoon chili flakes (adjust to taste)

Garnish (optional):

- Chopped cilantro
- Additional bean sprouts
- Red chili flakes

Instructions:

1. **Prepare the Rice Noodles:**
   - Soak the rice noodles in warm water for about 30 minutes, or according to package instructions, until they are pliable but still firm. Drain well before using.
2. **Make the Pad Thai Sauce:**
   - In a small bowl, whisk together tamarind paste, fish sauce, palm sugar, soy sauce, and chili flakes until well combined. Adjust sweetness or sourness to your taste by adding more sugar or tamarind paste if needed.
3. **Stir-Fry the Ingredients:**
   - Heat 1 tablespoon of vegetable oil in a wok or large skillet over medium-high heat. Add minced garlic and chopped shallot, and stir-fry for about 30 seconds until fragrant.

- Add shrimp and dried shrimp (if using), and stir-fry for 2-3 minutes until the shrimp turn pink and are cooked through. Push the shrimp to one side of the wok.
        - Add the beaten eggs to the empty side of the wok and scramble until just set.
4. **Add Noodles and Sauce:**
    - Add the soaked and drained rice noodles to the wok. Pour the prepared Pad Thai sauce over the noodles.
    - Use tongs or chopsticks to toss everything together, ensuring the noodles are evenly coated with the sauce. Stir-fry for 2-3 minutes until the noodles are tender and well combined with the other ingredients.
5. **Add Bean Sprouts and Spring Onions:**
    - Add bean sprouts and spring onions (reserve some for garnish if desired), and toss for another 1-2 minutes until the bean sprouts are slightly wilted but still crunchy.
6. **Serve:**
    - Transfer Pad Thai to serving plates. Sprinkle with chopped roasted peanuts and garnish with lime wedges on the side.
7. **Garnish and Serve:**
    - Garnish with additional bean sprouts, chopped cilantro, and red chili flakes if desired. Serve immediately with lime wedges on the side.

Tips:

- **Preparation:** Have all your ingredients prepped and ready to go as stir-frying happens quickly.
- **Adjustments:** Feel free to adjust the ingredients to suit your taste preferences, such as adding more chili flakes for spiciness or adjusting the sweetness of the sauce.
- **Variations:** Pad Thai is versatile; you can substitute shrimp with chicken, tofu, or keep it vegetarian by adding more vegetables like bell peppers or carrots.
- **Storage:** Pad Thai is best served fresh but can be stored in an airtight container in the refrigerator for up to 2 days. Reheat gently in a pan or microwave before serving.

Enjoy making this classic Thai dish at home—Pad Thai is sure to be a hit at your table with its delightful flavors and textures!

Thai Fish Congee (Jok Pla)

Ingredients:

- 1 cup jasmine rice, rinsed
- 6 cups water or chicken broth (or a combination)
- 200g white fish fillets (such as tilapia or cod), thinly sliced
- 1 tablespoon fish sauce
- 1 tablespoon soy sauce
- 1 teaspoon sugar
- 2-3 cloves garlic, minced
- 1-2 tablespoons ginger, finely grated
- 2-3 spring onions, thinly sliced
- 2 tablespoons cilantro leaves, chopped
- White pepper, to taste
- Fried garlic, for garnish (optional)
- Fried shallots, for garnish (optional)
- Boiled egg, halved, for serving (optional)
- Chili vinegar or chili sauce, for serving (optional)

Instructions:

1. **Cook the Rice:**
   - In a large pot, bring the water or chicken broth to a boil over medium-high heat. Add the rinsed jasmine rice and stir well. Reduce heat to medium-low and simmer, stirring occasionally, until the rice is soft and has broken down into a porridge consistency, about 30-40 minutes.
2. **Prepare the Fish:**
   - While the rice is cooking, season the fish fillets with fish sauce and set aside.
3. **Flavor the Congee:**
   - Once the rice is porridge-like, add the seasoned fish fillets to the pot. Stir gently to combine. Cook for an additional 5-7 minutes, or until the fish is cooked through and flakes easily with a fork.
4. **Season the Congee:**
   - Add soy sauce, sugar, minced garlic, and grated ginger to the congee. Stir well to incorporate the flavors. Taste and adjust seasoning as needed, adding more fish sauce or soy sauce for saltiness, or sugar for sweetness.
5. **Serve:**
   - Ladle the Jok Pla into serving bowls. Garnish with sliced spring onions, chopped cilantro, and a sprinkle of white pepper.
6. **Optional Garnishes:**
   - For extra flavor and texture, you can top the congee with fried garlic, fried shallots, or a boiled egg halved. Serve with chili vinegar or chili sauce on the side for those who enjoy a bit of heat.
7. **Enjoy:**

- Serve Jok Pla hot as a comforting breakfast or a light meal. It's traditionally enjoyed with a side of fresh herbs, such as Thai basil or cilantro, and additional condiments like chili vinegar for added zest.

Tips:

- **Consistency:** Adjust the amount of water or broth based on your preference for a thicker or thinner congee.
- **Fish:** Feel free to use any white fish fillets that you prefer or have on hand. Adjust cooking time accordingly based on the thickness of the fish.
- **Variations:** Some recipes include adding preserved salted eggs or century eggs for additional flavor. You can also add sliced mushrooms or vegetables like bok choy to the congee for added texture and nutrients.
- **Storage:** Congee stores well in the refrigerator for up to 3 days. Reheat gently on the stovetop or in the microwave, adding a little water or broth to adjust consistency if needed.

Jok Pla is a soothing and satisfying dish that's perfect for any time of the day, especially when you need something warm and comforting. Enjoy making and savoring this Thai fish congee at home!

Thai Chicken Curry with Rice Noodles (Khao Soi)

Ingredients:

For the Curry Paste:

- 4-6 dried red chilies, soaked in warm water for 15 minutes, drained, and chopped
- 4 cloves garlic, minced
- 1 shallot, chopped
- 1 thumb-sized piece of ginger, grated
- 1 tablespoon ground coriander
- 1 teaspoon ground turmeric
- 1/2 teaspoon ground cumin
- 1/2 teaspoon shrimp paste (optional)
- 1 tablespoon vegetable oil

For the Khao Soi:

- 1 tablespoon vegetable oil
- 1 pound boneless, skinless chicken thighs or breasts, thinly sliced
- 2 cups coconut milk
- 2 cups chicken broth
- 2 tablespoons soy sauce
- 1 tablespoon fish sauce
- 1 tablespoon palm sugar or brown sugar
- Salt, to taste
- 200g dried rice noodles, cooked according to package instructions
- Fresh cilantro leaves, chopped, for garnish
- Fresh lime wedges, for serving

Optional Toppings:

- Crispy fried noodles (often used in traditional Khao Soi)
- Sliced red onion
- Pickled mustard greens
- Roasted peanuts, chopped

Instructions:

1. **Prepare the Curry Paste:**
   - In a blender or food processor, combine soaked and chopped dried red chilies, minced garlic, chopped shallot, grated ginger, ground coriander, ground turmeric, ground cumin, and shrimp paste (if using). Blend until a smooth paste forms, adding a little vegetable oil if needed to help the blending process.
2. **Cook the Chicken:**

- Heat 1 tablespoon of vegetable oil in a large pot or Dutch oven over medium heat. Add the curry paste and sauté for 2-3 minutes until fragrant.
- Add thinly sliced chicken thighs or breasts to the pot. Cook, stirring occasionally, until the chicken is browned and cooked through.

3. **Add Coconut Milk and Broth:**
   - Pour in coconut milk and chicken broth, stirring to combine. Bring to a simmer over medium heat.
4. **Season the Curry:**
   - Stir in soy sauce, fish sauce, and palm sugar (or brown sugar). Taste and adjust seasoning with salt as needed. Simmer for 10-15 minutes to allow flavors to meld together.
5. **Prepare the Noodles:**
   - While the curry simmers, cook the rice noodles according to package instructions. Drain and set aside.
6. **Serve Khao Soi:**
   - Divide the cooked rice noodles among serving bowls. Ladle the hot curry broth and chicken over the noodles.
7. **Garnish and Serve:**
   - Garnish each bowl of Khao Soi with chopped fresh cilantro leaves. Serve with lime wedges on the side for squeezing over the curry.
8. **Optional Toppings:**
   - Top Khao Soi with crispy fried noodles, sliced red onion, pickled mustard greens, and chopped roasted peanuts for added texture and flavor.

Tips:

- **Curry Paste:** If you prefer a milder spice level, adjust the amount of dried red chilies used in the curry paste.
- **Chicken:** You can substitute chicken with beef, pork, or tofu for different variations of Khao Soi.
- **Storage:** Khao Soi leftovers can be stored in an airtight container in the refrigerator for up to 3 days. Reheat gently on the stovetop or in the microwave before serving.

Khao Soi is a flavorful and comforting Thai curry dish that combines the richness of coconut milk with the aromatic spices of the curry paste. Enjoy making and savoring this traditional Northern Thai dish at home!

Thai Spicy Pork Salad (Nam Tok Moo)

Ingredients:

For the Pork:

- 400g pork loin or pork shoulder, thinly sliced or cut into bite-sized pieces
- 1 tablespoon vegetable oil
- 1 tablespoon fish sauce
- 1 tablespoon soy sauce
- 1 teaspoon sugar
- 1/2 teaspoon ground white pepper

For the Salad:

- 1/4 cup thinly sliced shallots
- 1/4 cup chopped spring onions
- 2-3 tablespoons roasted rice powder (see Note below)
- 2-3 tablespoons fresh lime juice (about 1-2 limes)
- 2-3 tablespoons fish sauce (adjust to taste)
- 1 teaspoon chili flakes (adjust to taste)
- Fresh cilantro leaves, chopped, for garnish
- Fresh mint leaves, chopped, for garnish
- Fresh lettuce leaves, for serving

Optional Ingredients:

- 1-2 tablespoons toasted sticky rice powder (for extra texture and flavor)
- Sliced cucumber, for serving

Instructions:

1. **Prepare the Pork:**
    - If grilling, preheat the grill or grill pan over medium-high heat. Grill the pork slices or pieces for 3-4 minutes on each side until cooked through and slightly charred. Alternatively, you can boil the pork in water until fully cooked, then thinly slice it.
    - Once cooked, let the pork rest for a few minutes, then thinly slice it if not already sliced.
2. **Make the Dressing:**
    - In a mixing bowl, combine lime juice, fish sauce, sugar, and chili flakes. Stir until the sugar has dissolved.
3. **Assemble the Salad:**
    - In a large mixing bowl, combine the sliced pork, thinly sliced shallots, chopped spring onions, and roasted rice powder.

- Pour the dressing over the salad mixture. Toss gently to combine, ensuring the pork and vegetables are coated evenly with the dressing.

4. **Serve:**
   - Arrange fresh lettuce leaves on a serving platter. Spoon the Nam Tok Moo salad onto the lettuce leaves.
5. **Garnish:**
   - Garnish with chopped fresh cilantro and mint leaves. Optionally, sprinkle toasted sticky rice powder on top for added texture.
6. **Optional Serving:**
   - Serve with additional fresh herbs, sliced cucumber, and sticky rice on the side.

Notes:

- **Roasted Rice Powder:** To make roasted rice powder, dry-roast raw sticky rice in a pan over medium heat until golden brown and fragrant. Grind the roasted rice in a mortar and pestle or spice grinder until it becomes a fine powder. This adds a nutty flavor and enhances the texture of the salad.
- **Adjust Seasonings:** Taste the salad before serving and adjust the lime juice, fish sauce, and chili flakes to suit your preference for sweetness, saltiness, and spiciness.

Nam Tok Moo is a refreshing and zesty Thai salad that's perfect as a light main dish or appetizer. It's bursting with flavors from the tangy dressing and aromatic herbs, making it a favorite among Thai salad enthusiasts. Enjoy making and savoring this delicious Nam Tok Moo at home!

Thai Pork Satay (Moo Satay)

Ingredients:

For the Pork Satay:

- 500g pork loin or pork shoulder, thinly sliced or cut into strips
- 1 tablespoon vegetable oil
- 2 tablespoons soy sauce
- 2 tablespoons fish sauce
- 1 tablespoon curry powder
- 1 tablespoon turmeric powder
- 2 tablespoons coconut milk
- 1 tablespoon sugar
- Bamboo skewers, soaked in water for at least 30 minutes

For the Peanut Sauce:

- 1/2 cup creamy peanut butter
- 1/2 cup coconut milk
- 2 tablespoons soy sauce
- 1 tablespoon fish sauce
- 1 tablespoon brown sugar
- 1 tablespoon lime juice
- 1 teaspoon curry powder
- 1 teaspoon chili paste or sriracha (adjust to taste)
- Water (as needed to adjust consistency)

Optional Garnishes:

- Chopped cilantro
- Crushed peanuts
- Sliced cucumbers and red onions

Instructions:

1. **Marinate the Pork:**
   - In a bowl, combine vegetable oil, soy sauce, fish sauce, curry powder, turmeric powder, coconut milk, and sugar. Mix well to make a marinade.
   - Add the thinly sliced pork to the marinade, ensuring all pieces are coated. Cover and refrigerate for at least 1 hour, or ideally overnight, to let the flavors infuse.
2. **Make the Peanut Sauce:**
   - In a small saucepan over medium heat, combine peanut butter, coconut milk, soy sauce, fish sauce, brown sugar, lime juice, curry powder, and chili paste or sriracha.

- Stir continuously until the peanut butter melts and the sauce is smooth. If the sauce is too thick, thin it out with a little water until you reach your desired consistency. Remove from heat and set aside.
3. **Skewer and Grill the Pork:**
    - Preheat your grill or grill pan over medium-high heat. Thread the marinated pork slices onto soaked bamboo skewers.
    - Grill the pork skewers for about 3-4 minutes on each side, or until cooked through and nicely charred. Alternatively, you can broil them in the oven on a baking sheet lined with foil.
4. **Serve:**
    - Arrange the grilled Moo Satay skewers on a serving platter. Serve with the prepared peanut sauce on the side for dipping.
5. **Garnish and Enjoy:**
    - Garnish with chopped cilantro and crushed peanuts if desired. Serve Moo Satay with sliced cucumbers and red onions on the side.

Tips:

- **Marinating Time:** Marinating the pork overnight enhances the flavor, but marinating for at least 1 hour will still give good results.
- **Peanut Sauce Consistency:** Adjust the thickness of the peanut sauce by adding more coconut milk or water if needed.
- **Grilling Tips:** Ensure your grill or grill pan is hot before adding the skewers to achieve those beautiful grill marks and charred flavor.
- **Variations:** You can use chicken or beef instead of pork for different variations of satay.
- **Storage:** Leftover Moo Satay can be stored in an airtight container in the refrigerator for up to 3 days. Reheat gently in the oven or microwave before serving.

Thai Pork Satay (Moo Satay) is a fantastic appetizer or main dish that's perfect for gatherings and parties. Enjoy the delicious flavors of grilled pork skewers paired with creamy peanut sauce—it's sure to be a hit!

Thai Spicy Green Papaya Salad (Som Tum)

Ingredients:

- 1 small green papaya (about 500g), peeled, seeded, and julienned (use a julienne peeler or a knife)
- 2-3 cloves garlic, minced
- 2-3 Thai bird's eye chilies, finely chopped (adjust to taste)
- 2-3 cherry tomatoes, halved or quartered
- 2 tablespoons dried shrimp, soaked in water for 10 minutes and drained (optional)
- 2 tablespoons roasted peanuts, roughly chopped
- 2 tablespoons fish sauce
- 1-2 tablespoons palm sugar or brown sugar (adjust to taste)
- 2 tablespoons lime juice (about 1-2 limes)
- 1-2 tablespoons tamarind juice or tamarind concentrate (adjust to taste)
- Fresh cilantro leaves, chopped, for garnish
- Fresh lettuce leaves, for serving

Instructions:

1. **Prepare the Green Papaya:**
   - Peel the green papaya, cut it in half lengthwise, and scoop out the seeds. Julienne the papaya into thin strips using a julienne peeler or a sharp knife. Place the julienned papaya in a large mixing bowl.
2. **Make the Dressing:**
   - In a small bowl, combine minced garlic, chopped Thai chilies, fish sauce, palm sugar, lime juice, and tamarind juice or concentrate. Mix well until the sugar dissolves and all ingredients are incorporated. Adjust the flavors to your liking by adding more fish sauce for saltiness, sugar for sweetness, lime juice for acidity, or chilies for spiciness.
3. **Assemble the Salad:**
   - Add cherry tomatoes, soaked dried shrimp (if using), and half of the chopped roasted peanuts to the julienned green papaya.
   - Pour the dressing over the salad ingredients in the bowl.
4. **Toss and Serve:**
   - Toss everything together gently using tongs or clean hands, ensuring the papaya is evenly coated with the dressing.
5. **Garnish and Serve:**
   - Transfer the Som Tum to a serving plate or bowl lined with fresh lettuce leaves.
   - Garnish with the remaining chopped roasted peanuts and chopped cilantro leaves.

Tips:

- **Green Papaya:** Look for a green papaya that is firm and unripe. It should have green skin without any yellow or orange patches.
- **Thai Chilies:** Adjust the amount of Thai chilies according to your spice preference. Be cautious as they are very spicy!
- **Dried Shrimp:** Dried shrimp adds a traditional umami flavor to Som Tum. If you prefer a vegetarian version, you can omit it.
- **Serve Chilled:** Som Tum is best served chilled, making it a refreshing dish on a hot day.
- **Variations:** Some variations of Som Tum include adding green beans, carrots, or crab meat. Feel free to customize the salad to your taste.

Som Tum is a quintessential Thai salad that balances sweet, sour, salty, and spicy flavors in a delightful way. Enjoy making and savoring this classic Thai dish at home!

Thai Stir-Fried Morning Glory (Pad Pak Boong)

Ingredients:

- 1 bunch of morning glory (about 300g), washed and trimmed
- 2-3 cloves garlic, minced
- 2-3 Thai bird's eye chilies, finely chopped (adjust to taste)
- 1 tablespoon oyster sauce
- 1 tablespoon soy sauce
- 1/2 tablespoon fish sauce
- 1/2 teaspoon sugar
- 1 tablespoon vegetable oil
- Optional: sliced shallots for garnish

Instructions:

1. **Prepare the Morning Glory:**
   - Wash the morning glory thoroughly under cold water. Trim off any tough stems and separate the leaves and tender stems from the thicker stems. Cut into manageable lengths, about 3 inches long.
2. **Make the Sauce:**
   - In a small bowl, mix together oyster sauce, soy sauce, fish sauce, and sugar. Stir well to dissolve the sugar.
3. **Stir-Fry the Morning Glory:**
   - Heat vegetable oil in a wok or large skillet over medium-high heat. Add minced garlic and chopped Thai chilies. Stir-fry for about 30 seconds until fragrant, being careful not to burn the garlic.
   - Add the morning glory to the wok. Stir-fry continuously for 1-2 minutes until the leaves start to wilt and the stems become tender-crisp.
4. **Add the Sauce:**
   - Pour the prepared sauce over the morning glory in the wok. Stir-fry for another 1-2 minutes, ensuring the morning glory is evenly coated with the sauce.
5. **Serve:**
   - Transfer the Pad Pak Boong to a serving plate. Garnish with sliced shallots if desired.

Tips:

- **Morning Glory:** Choose fresh morning glory with vibrant green leaves and tender stems. If morning glory is not available, you can substitute with other leafy greens like spinach or kale.
- **Thai Chilies:** Adjust the amount of Thai chilies according to your spice preference. Be cautious as they are very spicy!

- **Stir-Frying:** Stir-fry quickly over high heat to retain the vibrant green color and crisp texture of the morning glory.
- **Variations:** Some variations include adding sliced bell peppers, mushrooms, or tofu for added texture and flavor.
- **Serve With:** Pad Pak Boong is typically served alongside steamed rice as a side dish or part of a larger Thai meal.

Pad Pak Boong is a quick and flavorful dish that showcases the fresh and delicate flavors of morning glory. Enjoy making and savoring this Thai stir-fry at home!

Thai Grilled Chicken (Gai Yang)

Ingredients:

For the Marinade:

- 1.5 kg chicken pieces (such as thighs, drumsticks, or breast)
- 4 cloves garlic, minced
- 2 tablespoons cilantro roots or stems, finely chopped (or use cilantro leaves if roots are not available)
- 2 tablespoons fish sauce
- 2 tablespoons soy sauce
- 2 tablespoons oyster sauce
- 2 tablespoons palm sugar or brown sugar
- 1 tablespoon ground coriander
- 1 teaspoon ground turmeric
- 1/2 teaspoon white pepper

For Serving:

- Sticky rice, for serving (optional)
- Thai sweet chili sauce, for dipping (optional)
- Sliced cucumbers, for garnish (optional)

Instructions:

1. **Prepare the Marinade:**
   - In a bowl, combine minced garlic, chopped cilantro roots or stems, fish sauce, soy sauce, oyster sauce, palm sugar or brown sugar, ground coriander, ground turmeric, and white pepper. Mix well until the sugar is dissolved and the marinade is well combined.
2. **Marinate the Chicken:**
   - Place the chicken pieces in a large bowl or resealable plastic bag. Pour the marinade over the chicken, making sure each piece is well coated. Marinate in the refrigerator for at least 2 hours, or ideally overnight, to allow the flavors to penetrate the meat.
3. **Grill the Chicken:**
   - Preheat your grill to medium-high heat. If using charcoal, prepare it for direct grilling.
   - Remove the chicken from the marinade, shaking off any excess. Reserve the marinade for basting.
   - Grill the chicken pieces for about 5-7 minutes on each side, or until fully cooked and nicely charred. Baste with the reserved marinade occasionally during grilling to keep the chicken moist and flavorful.
4. **Serve:**

- Transfer the grilled Gai Yang to a serving platter. Serve immediately with sticky rice, Thai sweet chili sauce for dipping, and sliced cucumbers on the side.

Tips:

- **Chicken Cuts:** You can use a variety of chicken cuts for Gai Yang. Thighs and drumsticks are popular choices as they stay juicy and flavorful on the grill.
- **Grilling:** Ensure your grill is well preheated before adding the chicken to achieve those beautiful grill marks and smoky flavor. If using a charcoal grill, the chicken should be cooked over direct heat.
- **Sticky Rice:** Sticky rice (also known as glutinous rice) is a traditional accompaniment to Gai Yang. It complements the flavors and helps balance the spiciness.
- **Variations:** Some recipes include lemongrass or ginger in the marinade for additional aromatic flavors. Feel free to adjust the marinade ingredients to suit your taste preferences.
- **Leftovers:** Leftover Gai Yang can be refrigerated in an airtight container for up to 3 days. Reheat gently in the oven or microwave before serving.

Gai Yang is a delicious and aromatic Thai grilled chicken dish that's perfect for any occasion, whether as a main course or part of a Thai-inspired barbecue. Enjoy making and savoring this flavorful street food classic at home!

Thai Grilled Pork Skewers (Moo Ping)

Ingredients:

For the Pork Skewers:

- 500g pork loin or pork shoulder, thinly sliced or cut into bite-sized pieces
- Bamboo skewers, soaked in water for at least 30 minutes

For the Marinade:

- 3 cloves garlic, minced
- 1 tablespoon cilantro roots or stems, finely chopped (or use cilantro leaves if roots are not available)
- 2 tablespoons soy sauce
- 2 tablespoons oyster sauce
- 2 tablespoons fish sauce
- 1 tablespoon palm sugar or brown sugar
- 1 tablespoon ground coriander
- 1 tablespoon ground turmeric
- 1/2 teaspoon ground white pepper

For Serving:

- Sticky rice or steamed jasmine rice
- Thai sweet chili sauce, for dipping (optional)
- Sliced cucumbers and red onions, for garnish (optional)

Instructions:

1. **Prepare the Marinade:**
   - In a bowl, combine minced garlic, chopped cilantro roots or stems, soy sauce, oyster sauce, fish sauce, palm sugar or brown sugar, ground coriander, ground turmeric, and ground white pepper. Mix well until the sugar is dissolved and the marinade is well combined.
2. **Marinate the Pork:**
   - Add the thinly sliced or bite-sized pork pieces to the marinade. Toss to coat the pork evenly. Cover and refrigerate for at least 2 hours, or ideally overnight, to allow the flavors to meld together.
3. **Skewer the Pork:**
   - Preheat your grill or grill pan over medium-high heat. Thread the marinated pork pieces onto soaked bamboo skewers, leaving a bit of space between each piece.
4. **Grill the Pork Skewers:**

- Grill the Moo Ping skewers for about 3-4 minutes on each side, or until the pork is fully cooked and nicely charred. Baste with any remaining marinade or oil occasionally during grilling to keep the pork moist and flavorful.
5. **Serve:**
    - Transfer the grilled Moo Ping skewers to a serving platter. Serve immediately with sticky rice or steamed jasmine rice.
6. **Optional Garnishes:**
    - Serve with Thai sweet chili sauce for dipping, and garnish with sliced cucumbers and red onions on the side.

Tips:

- **Pork Cuts:** Pork loin or pork shoulder are commonly used for Moo Ping due to their tenderness and flavor. Ensure the pieces are thinly sliced or cut into bite-sized pieces for even cooking.
- **Grilling Tips:** Preheat your grill well before adding the skewers to achieve those beautiful grill marks and charred flavor. If using a charcoal grill, cook the skewers over direct heat.
- **Variations:** Some recipes include coconut milk in the marinade for added richness. You can also adjust the spiciness by adding chopped Thai chilies or chili flakes to the marinade.
- **Serve With:** Moo Ping is traditionally served with sticky rice or steamed jasmine rice, providing a balanced and satisfying meal.
- **Leftovers:** Any leftover Moo Ping can be stored in an airtight container in the refrigerator for up to 3 days. Reheat gently in the oven or microwave before serving.

Enjoy making and savoring these delicious Thai Grilled Pork Skewers (Moo Ping) at home! They make a fantastic appetizer or main dish that captures the authentic flavors of Thai street food.

Thai Stir-Fried Rice Noodles (Pad See Ew)

Ingredients:

- 200g wide rice noodles (sen yai), fresh or dried
- 200g chicken breast, thinly sliced (or substitute with beef, pork, shrimp, or tofu)
- 2 cups Chinese broccoli (gai lan) or regular broccoli, cut into bite-sized pieces
- 2-3 cloves garlic, minced
- 2 eggs, beaten
- 2 tablespoons soy sauce
- 1 tablespoon oyster sauce
- 1 tablespoon dark soy sauce (for color and depth of flavor)
- 1 tablespoon fish sauce
- 1 tablespoon sugar (palm sugar or brown sugar)
- 1/4 cup chicken broth or water
- Vegetable oil for cooking
- White pepper, to taste
- Fresh cilantro leaves and sliced lime, for garnish (optional)

Instructions:

1. **Prepare the Rice Noodles:**
   - If using dried rice noodles, soak them in warm water for about 30 minutes until they are pliable but still firm. If using fresh noodles, separate them gently with your fingers.
2. **Prepare the Sauce:**
   - In a small bowl, mix together soy sauce, oyster sauce, dark soy sauce, fish sauce, and sugar until well combined. Set aside.
3. **Stir-Fry the Chicken (or Protein):**
   - Heat 1 tablespoon of vegetable oil in a wok or large skillet over medium-high heat. Add minced garlic and stir-fry for about 30 seconds until fragrant.
   - Add the sliced chicken (or your choice of protein) to the wok. Stir-fry until the chicken is cooked through. If using shrimp, cook until they turn pink and opaque.
4. **Cook the Vegetables:**
   - Push the chicken to the side of the wok. Add a little more oil if needed, then crack the eggs into the empty space. Scramble the eggs until they are cooked through, then mix them with the chicken.
   - Add Chinese broccoli (or regular broccoli) to the wok. Stir-fry for another 1-2 minutes until the broccoli is tender-crisp.
5. **Add the Noodles and Sauce:**
   - Add the soaked rice noodles to the wok. Pour the prepared sauce over the noodles. Use tongs or chopsticks to gently toss everything together, ensuring the noodles are evenly coated with the sauce.
6. **Finish Cooking:**
   - Pour chicken broth or water around the edges of the wok. Stir-fry for another 2-3 minutes until the noodles are tender and everything is heated through. Adjust

seasoning with more soy sauce or fish sauce if needed. Sprinkle with white pepper to taste.

7. **Serve:**
   - Transfer Pad See Ew to serving plates. Garnish with fresh cilantro leaves and sliced lime if desired.

Tips:

- **Rice Noodles:** Use wide rice noodles (sen yai) for an authentic texture. If unavailable, you can substitute with wide rice sticks or pad Thai noodles.
- **Vegetables:** Chinese broccoli (gai lan) is traditional, but regular broccoli works well too. You can also add sliced carrots or bell peppers for extra color and crunch.
- **Dark Soy Sauce:** This adds color and a richer flavor to the dish. If you don't have dark soy sauce, you can use regular soy sauce but the color won't be as deep.
- **Cooking Technique:** Stir-fry quickly over high heat to maintain the freshness and texture of the noodles and vegetables.
- **Customization:** Feel free to adjust the sweetness (with more sugar), saltiness (with more soy sauce or fish sauce), or spiciness (with chili flakes or fresh Thai chilies) to suit your taste.

Pad See Ew is a comforting and satisfying Thai noodle dish that's perfect for lunch or dinner. Enjoy making and savoring this delicious dish at home!

Thai Red Curry with Rice (Khao Pad Prik Gaeng)

Ingredients:

- 1 cup jasmine rice, cooked and cooled (preferably day-old rice)
- 200g chicken breast or thigh, thinly sliced (or substitute with beef, pork, shrimp, tofu)
- 2-3 tablespoons Thai red curry paste
- 1 cup mixed vegetables (such as bell peppers, carrots, broccoli)
- 1 cup coconut milk
- 1 tablespoon fish sauce
- 1 tablespoon soy sauce
- 1 tablespoon palm sugar or brown sugar
- 2 kaffir lime leaves, thinly sliced (optional)
- Fresh Thai basil leaves, for garnish (optional)
- Vegetable oil for cooking

Instructions:

1. **Prepare the Rice:**
    - Cook jasmine rice according to package instructions. For best results, use day-old rice that has been cooled in the refrigerator. This helps to prevent the rice from becoming mushy during stir-frying.
2. **Stir-Fry the Chicken (or Protein):**
    - Heat 1 tablespoon of vegetable oil in a wok or large skillet over medium-high heat. Add sliced chicken (or your choice of protein) and stir-fry until cooked through. Remove from the wok and set aside.
3. **Cook the Curry Base:**
    - In the same wok, add another tablespoon of oil if needed. Add Thai red curry paste and stir-fry for about 1 minute until fragrant.
    - Pour in coconut milk and stir to combine with the curry paste. Let it simmer for a few minutes until the oil starts to separate and the sauce thickens slightly.
4. **Add Vegetables and Seasoning:**
    - Add mixed vegetables to the wok. Stir-fry for 2-3 minutes until they are tender-crisp.
    - Season with fish sauce, soy sauce, and palm sugar (or brown sugar). Stir well to combine.
5. **Combine with Rice:**
    - Add the cooked jasmine rice to the wok. Gently toss everything together, ensuring the rice is well coated with the curry sauce and vegetables.
6. **Finish and Serve:**
    - Return the cooked chicken (or protein) to the wok. Stir-fry for another minute until everything is heated through.
    - Remove from heat and garnish with thinly sliced kaffir lime leaves and fresh Thai basil leaves, if using.
7. **Serve:**
    - Transfer Khao Pad Prik Gaeng to serving plates or bowls. Serve hot and enjoy!

Tips:

- **Thai Red Curry Paste:** Use store-bought Thai red curry paste or make your own for authentic flavors. Adjust the amount according to your spice preference.
- **Protein Options:** Feel free to substitute chicken with beef, pork, shrimp, or tofu. Adjust cooking times accordingly.
- **Vegetables:** Use your favorite vegetables or whatever you have on hand. Bell peppers, carrots, and broccoli work well in this dish.
- **Rice Texture:** Using day-old rice helps to maintain a firm texture. If using freshly cooked rice, spread it out on a baking sheet to cool quickly before stir-frying.
- **Garnishes:** Fresh Thai basil leaves and thinly sliced kaffir lime leaves add a refreshing aroma and flavor to the dish.

Khao Pad Prik Gaeng is a flavorful and satisfying Thai dish that combines the richness of red curry with the comfort of rice. Enjoy making this delicious meal at home!

Thai Sweet Coconut Soup (Tub Tim Grob)

Ingredients:

For the Water Chestnuts:

- 200g water chestnuts, peeled and cubed into small pieces
- Red food coloring (optional)
- Green food coloring (optional)

For the Syrup:

- 1 cup coconut milk
- 1/2 cup water
- 1/2 cup palm sugar or granulated sugar
- 1/4 teaspoon salt

For Serving:

- Crushed ice

Optional Garnishes:

- Jackfruit slices (fresh or canned)
- Sweetened coconut strips (optional)

Instructions:

1. **Prepare the Water Chestnuts:**
   - Peel the water chestnuts and cut them into small cubes. You can optionally color them with red and green food coloring to add a festive touch.
2. **Make the Syrup:**
   - In a saucepan, combine coconut milk, water, palm sugar (or granulated sugar), and salt. Stir over medium heat until the sugar has dissolved and the mixture is well combined. Bring to a gentle simmer.
3. **Cook the Water Chestnuts:**
   - Add the cubed water chestnuts to the simmering coconut syrup. Cook for about 5-7 minutes, stirring occasionally, until the water chestnuts are tender and translucent.
4. **Chill the Mixture:**
   - Remove the pan from heat and let the mixture cool to room temperature. Then, transfer it to the refrigerator and chill for at least 1 hour, or until ready to serve.
5. **Serve:**
   - To serve, place a generous amount of crushed ice in serving bowls or glasses.
   - Spoon the chilled water chestnuts and coconut milk syrup over the crushed ice.
6. **Optional Garnishes:**
   - Garnish with slices of jackfruit and sweetened coconut strips if desired.
7. **Enjoy:**
   - Serve Tub Tim Grob immediately and enjoy this refreshing Thai dessert!

Tips:

- **Water Chestnuts:** Fresh water chestnuts are ideal for this dessert. If using canned water chestnuts, rinse them thoroughly before using.
- **Coloring:** Food coloring is optional but adds a vibrant color contrast to the dessert.
- **Coconut Milk:** Use full-fat coconut milk for a rich and creamy texture. You can adjust the sweetness of the syrup to your preference by adding more or less sugar.
- **Make Ahead:** You can prepare the water chestnuts and syrup ahead of time and assemble the dessert just before serving to keep the crushed ice from melting too quickly.

Tub Tim Grob is a popular Thai dessert that combines the sweetness of coconut milk with the refreshing crunch of water chestnuts. Enjoy making and serving this delightful treat to impress your guests or satisfy your sweet tooth!

Thai Stir-Fried Eggplant (Pad Makua Yao)

Ingredients:

- 2 medium-sized Asian eggplants (long purple variety), cut into thick batons or wedges
- 3 cloves garlic, minced
- 2-3 Thai bird's eye chilies, thinly sliced (adjust to taste)
- 2 tablespoons oyster sauce
- 1 tablespoon soy sauce
- 1 tablespoon fish sauce
- 1 teaspoon sugar
- 1/4 cup chicken broth or water
- Vegetable oil for cooking
- Fresh Thai basil leaves or cilantro leaves, for garnish (optional)

Instructions:

1. **Prepare the Eggplants:**
   - Cut the Asian eggplants into thick batons or wedges, about 1-inch in width. You can optionally soak them in lightly salted water for 10-15 minutes to reduce bitterness, then drain and pat dry with paper towels.
2. **Make the Sauce:**
   - In a small bowl, mix together oyster sauce, soy sauce, fish sauce, and sugar until well combined. Set aside.
3. **Stir-Fry the Eggplant:**
   - Heat 2 tablespoons of vegetable oil in a wok or large skillet over medium-high heat.
   - Add minced garlic and sliced Thai bird's eye chilies. Stir-fry for about 30 seconds until fragrant.
   - Add the eggplant pieces to the wok. Stir-fry for about 2-3 minutes until they start to soften and brown slightly.
4. **Add the Sauce:**
   - Pour the prepared sauce over the eggplants in the wok. Stir to coat the eggplants evenly with the sauce.
5. **Cook Until Tender:**
   - Add chicken broth or water to the wok to create steam and help cook the eggplants further. Stir-fry for another 3-4 minutes or until the eggplants are tender and cooked through. Adjust the heat as needed to prevent burning.
6. **Garnish and Serve:**
   - Remove from heat. Garnish with fresh Thai basil leaves or cilantro leaves if desired.
7. **Serve:**
   - Transfer Pad Makua Yao to a serving plate or bowl. Serve hot as a side dish or part of a Thai meal with steamed jasmine rice.

Tips:

- **Eggplants:** Asian eggplants (long purple variety) are preferred for their tender texture and mild flavor. You can also use other varieties of eggplants, adjusting the cooking time as needed.
- **Chilies:** Adjust the amount of Thai bird's eye chilies according to your spice preference. Be cautious as they are very spicy.
- **Vegetarian Option:** Omit the oyster sauce and use vegetarian oyster sauce or mushroom sauce for a vegetarian version.
- **Variations:** Some recipes include adding sliced bell peppers, onions, or basil leaves for added flavor and texture.
- **Cooking Technique:** Stir-fry over medium-high heat to ensure the eggplants cook quickly and evenly without becoming mushy.

Pad Makua Yao is a delicious and comforting Thai dish that highlights the natural flavors of eggplants with a savory sauce. Enjoy making and savoring this flavorful stir-fry at home!

Thai Chicken and Rice Soup (Khao Man Gai)

Ingredients:

- 2 boneless, skinless chicken breasts
- 4 cups chicken broth (preferably low sodium)
- 1 cup jasmine rice (or other long-grain rice)
- 2-3 cloves garlic, minced
- 1-inch piece of ginger, grated
- 2-3 tablespoons soy sauce
- 1 tablespoon fish sauce
- 1 tablespoon vegetable oil
- 2-3 green onions, thinly sliced
- Fresh cilantro, chopped (for garnish)
- Lime wedges (for serving)
- Salt and pepper to taste

Instructions:

1. **Cook the Chicken:**
   - Season the chicken breasts with salt and pepper.
   - In a pot, bring water to a boil. Add the chicken breasts and cook for about 10-15 minutes until they are cooked through. Remove the chicken from the pot and shred it into small pieces.
2. **Prepare the Broth:**
   - In a large pot, heat the vegetable oil over medium heat.
   - Add the minced garlic and grated ginger, and sauté for about 1-2 minutes until fragrant.
   - Pour in the chicken broth and bring it to a simmer.
3. **Add Rice and Flavorings:**
   - Add the jasmine rice to the pot and stir well.
   - Season with soy sauce and fish sauce, adjusting the amounts to taste.
4. **Simmer:**
   - Reduce the heat to low, cover the pot, and let it simmer for about 15-20 minutes, or until the rice is cooked through and tender.
5. **Combine Chicken and Serve:**
   - Add the shredded chicken back into the pot and stir well to combine.
   - Taste and adjust seasoning with salt, pepper, soy sauce, or fish sauce if needed.
6. **Serve:**
   - Ladle the soup into bowls.
   - Garnish with sliced green onions and chopped cilantro.
   - Serve hot with lime wedges on the side for squeezing over the soup.

Notes:

- **Variations:** You can customize this soup by adding vegetables like sliced mushrooms, bok choy, or spinach during the cooking process.
- **Spice Level:** Adjust the spiciness by adding chili sauce or chili flakes if desired.
- **Storage:** Store any leftovers in an airtight container in the refrigerator for up to 3 days. Reheat gently on the stove or in the microwave.

Enjoy your homemade Thai Chicken and Rice Soup (Khao Man Gai) for a comforting and satisfying meal!

Thai Mango Sticky Rice (Khao Niew Mamuang)

Ingredients:

- 1 cup glutinous rice (also called sweet rice or sticky rice)
- 1 can (13.5 oz) coconut milk
- 1/2 cup sugar
- 1/2 teaspoon salt
- 2 ripe mangoes
- Toasted sesame seeds (optional, for garnish)

Instructions:

1. **Prepare the Sticky Rice:**
   - Rinse the glutinous rice under cold water until the water runs clear.
   - Soak the rice in water for at least 4 hours, or preferably overnight.
2. **Steam the Sticky Rice:**
   - Drain the soaked rice.
   - Line a steamer basket with cheesecloth or a clean cloth, and place the rice on top.
   - Steam the rice over medium-high heat for about 20-25 minutes, or until the rice is tender and cooked through.
3. **Prepare the Coconut Sauce:**
   - In a saucepan, combine the coconut milk, sugar, and salt.
   - Heat over medium heat, stirring constantly, until the sugar dissolves and the mixture is smooth and slightly thickened. Do not boil.
4. **Combine Sticky Rice and Coconut Sauce:**
   - Transfer the cooked sticky rice to a large bowl.
   - Pour about 3/4 of the warm coconut sauce over the rice, reserving the rest for serving.
   - Mix well until the rice is evenly coated with the coconut sauce. Let it sit for about 10-15 minutes to allow the flavors to meld.
5. **Prepare the Mangoes:**
   - Peel the mangoes and slice them into thin strips or cubes.
6. **Assemble:**
   - Serve the sticky rice on a plate or in a bowl.
   - Arrange the sliced mangoes alongside or on top of the rice.
   - Drizzle the remaining coconut sauce over the mangoes and rice.
   - Sprinkle with toasted sesame seeds for garnish, if desired.
7. **Serve:**
   - Serve the Mango Sticky Rice warm or at room temperature.

Notes:

- **Variations:** Some versions of this dessert include a pinch of salt in the coconut sauce or topping the dish with crispy mung beans for added texture.
- **Storage:** If you have leftovers, store the sticky rice, mangoes, and coconut sauce separately in the refrigerator. Reheat gently or enjoy cold.
- **Ripeness of Mangoes:** Choose ripe and fragrant mangoes for the best flavor. They should be slightly soft to the touch.

Enjoy your homemade Thai Mango Sticky Rice (Khao Niew Mamuang) for a delightful and authentic Thai dessert experience!

Thai Steamed Dumplings with Peanut Sauce (Khanom Jeeb Sai)

Ingredients:

For the Dumplings:

- 1/2 lb ground pork
- 1/2 lb shrimp, peeled, deveined, and finely chopped
- 2-3 water chestnuts, finely chopped (optional, for crunch)
- 2 cloves garlic, minced
- 1 tablespoon soy sauce
- 1 tablespoon oyster sauce
- 1/2 teaspoon sugar
- 1/4 teaspoon white pepper
- 1 tablespoon cornstarch
- 1 package round dumpling wrappers (about 50 wrappers)
- Cooking oil, for brushing

For the Peanut Dipping Sauce:

- 1/2 cup unsweetened coconut milk
- 3 tablespoons smooth peanut butter
- 1 tablespoon soy sauce
- 1 tablespoon rice vinegar or white vinegar
- 1 tablespoon sugar
- 1/2 teaspoon red chili flakes (optional, for heat)
- 1 clove garlic, minced
- Water, as needed to adjust consistency

Instructions:

1. **Prepare the Filling:**
   - In a mixing bowl, combine the ground pork, chopped shrimp, water chestnuts (if using), minced garlic, soy sauce, oyster sauce, sugar, white pepper, and cornstarch. Mix well until everything is evenly incorporated.
2. **Assemble the Dumplings:**
   - Take a dumpling wrapper and place a teaspoon of filling in the center.
   - Wet the edges of the wrapper with water using your finger.
   - Fold the wrapper in half and pinch the edges together to seal, creating a half-moon shape. You can also pleat the edges for a decorative touch.
3. **Steam the Dumplings:**
   - Arrange the dumplings on a lightly oiled steamer basket or tray, making sure they are not touching each other.
   - Steam the dumplings over high heat for about 8-10 minutes, or until the filling is cooked through and the wrappers are translucent.

4. **Make the Peanut Dipping Sauce:**
    - In a small saucepan, combine the coconut milk, peanut butter, soy sauce, rice vinegar, sugar, red chili flakes (if using), and minced garlic.
    - Heat over medium-low heat, stirring constantly, until the peanut butter is melted and the sauce is smooth. If the sauce is too thick, you can thin it out with a little water.
5. **Serve:**
    - Transfer the steamed dumplings to a serving plate.
    - Serve warm with the peanut dipping sauce on the side for dipping.

Notes:

- **Variations:** You can customize the filling by adding chopped cilantro, grated ginger, or finely chopped mushrooms for additional flavor.
- **Storage:** Leftover dumplings can be stored in an airtight container in the refrigerator for up to 2 days. Reheat gently in a steamer or microwave before serving.
- **Presentation:** Garnish the dumplings with chopped peanuts and fresh cilantro for added texture and color.

Enjoy your homemade Thai Steamed Dumplings with Peanut Sauce (Khanom Jeeb Sai) as a delicious appetizer or snack!

Thai Steamed Fish Custard (Hor Mok)

Ingredients:

- 1 lb firm white fish fillets (such as cod or tilapia), finely chopped or ground
- 1 cup coconut milk
- 2-3 tablespoons red curry paste (adjust to taste)
- 2 eggs
- 1 tablespoon fish sauce
- 1 tablespoon palm sugar or brown sugar
- 1 tablespoon cornstarch
- 1 kaffir lime leaf, finely shredded (optional)
- 1/4 cup Thai basil leaves, chopped (optional)
- Fresh red chili slices, for garnish (optional)
- Banana leaves or foil, for wrapping and steaming

Instructions:

1. **Prepare the Fish Mixture:**
   - In a bowl, combine the finely chopped fish, coconut milk, red curry paste, fish sauce, and palm sugar. Mix well until everything is evenly combined.
2. **Add Eggs and Thickener:**
   - Beat the eggs in a separate bowl.
   - Gradually add the beaten eggs to the fish mixture, stirring continuously.
   - Add the cornstarch and mix well to ensure the mixture is smooth and well combined.
3. **Prepare Banana Leaves (or Foil):**
   - If using banana leaves, briefly pass them over an open flame to soften them and make them more pliable. Cut into squares (about 6-8 inches).
4. **Assemble and Steam:**
   - Place a piece of banana leaf (or foil) in a small bowl or ramekin to create a cup shape.
   - Spoon the fish mixture into the cups, filling them about 3/4 full.
   - If using, sprinkle some shredded kaffir lime leaf and chopped Thai basil over the top for extra flavor.
5. **Steam the Custards:**
   - Prepare a steamer and steam the custard cups over medium-high heat for about 20-25 minutes, or until the custards are set and cooked through. The custards will firm up and become slightly translucent when done.
6. **Serve:**
   - Carefully remove the custard cups from the steamer.
   - Garnish with fresh red chili slices and additional Thai basil leaves, if desired.
   - Serve hot with steamed jasmine rice.

Notes:

- **Variations:** You can add additional vegetables like sliced bell peppers or Thai eggplants to the fish mixture for added texture and flavor.
- **Substitutions:** If banana leaves are not available, you can use aluminum foil to wrap the custards. Make sure to create a tight seal to retain moisture during steaming.
- **Storage:** Leftover custards can be stored in the refrigerator for up to 2 days. Reheat gently in a steamer or microwave before serving.

Enjoy your homemade Thai Steamed Fish Custard (Hor Mok) as a delightful and aromatic dish that showcases the rich flavors of Thai cuisine!

Thai Cucumber Relish (Ajat)

Ingredients:

- 1 large cucumber, thinly sliced or julienned
- 1/2 cup shallots, thinly sliced
- 1/2 cup fresh coriander (cilantro) leaves, chopped
- 1/2 cup roasted peanuts, roughly chopped
- 1/2 cup vinegar (rice vinegar or white vinegar)
- 1/4 cup water
- 1/4 cup sugar
- 1 teaspoon salt
- 1-2 Thai bird's eye chilies, thinly sliced (optional, for heat)

Instructions:

1. **Prepare the Cucumber Mixture:**
   - In a bowl, combine the thinly sliced cucumber, sliced shallots, chopped coriander leaves, and chopped roasted peanuts. Mix well.
2. **Make the Pickling Liquid:**
   - In a small saucepan, combine the vinegar, water, sugar, and salt.
   - Bring the mixture to a boil over medium-high heat, stirring occasionally until the sugar and salt dissolve completely.
   - Remove from heat and let the pickling liquid cool to room temperature.
3. **Combine and Chill:**
   - Pour the cooled pickling liquid over the cucumber mixture.
   - Add the sliced Thai bird's eye chilies, if using, for a spicy kick.
   - Stir gently to combine all the ingredients.
4. **Chill and Serve:**
   - Cover the bowl with plastic wrap or transfer the Ajat to a sealed container.
   - Refrigerate for at least 1 hour to allow the flavors to meld together.
5. **Serve:**
   - Stir the Ajat before serving.
   - Serve chilled as a side dish or condiment with your favorite Thai dishes, such as curries, grilled meats, or noodles.

Notes:

- **Variations:** You can adjust the sweetness or tanginess of the relish by varying the amount of sugar and vinegar according to your taste.
- **Storage:** Ajat can be stored in the refrigerator for up to 3 days. The flavors will continue to develop over time.
- **Presentation:** Garnish with additional chopped peanuts or coriander leaves before serving for added texture and freshness.

Enjoy your homemade Thai Cucumber Relish (Ajat) as a zesty and crunchy accompaniment that enhances the flavors of your meal!

Thai Fried Taro Dumplings (Khanom Phing)

Ingredients:

For the Filling:

- 1 cup taro root, peeled and grated
- 1/2 cup ground pork or chicken
- 1/4 cup dried shrimp, soaked and finely chopped
- 2-3 shallots, finely chopped
- 2 cloves garlic, minced
- 1 tablespoon fish sauce
- 1 tablespoon soy sauce
- 1 teaspoon sugar
- 1/2 teaspoon white pepper
- Cooking oil, for frying

For the Wrappers:

- Spring roll wrappers or rice paper wrappers
- Water, for sealing wrappers

Instructions:

1. **Prepare the Filling:**
    - Heat a bit of oil in a pan over medium heat.
    - Add the minced garlic and chopped shallots. Saute until fragrant.
    - Add the ground pork or chicken, breaking it up with a spatula, and cook until browned.
    - Add the grated taro root and dried shrimp. Cook for a few minutes until the taro starts to soften.
    - Season with fish sauce, soy sauce, sugar, and white pepper. Stir well to combine.
    - Remove from heat and let the filling cool completely.
2. **Assemble the Dumplings:**
    - Take a piece of spring roll wrapper or rice paper wrapper and place a spoonful of the cooled filling in the center.
    - Fold the wrapper over the filling to form a rectangle or triangle shape. Use water to seal the edges by brushing it along the edges and pressing firmly to seal.
3. **Fry the Dumplings:**
    - Heat cooking oil in a frying pan or wok over medium-high heat.
    - Carefully place the dumplings in the hot oil, a few at a time, without overcrowding.
    - Fry until golden brown and crispy on all sides, turning occasionally to ensure even cooking.

- Remove the fried dumplings with a slotted spoon and drain on paper towels to remove excess oil.
4. **Serve:**
    - Serve the fried taro dumplings (Khanom Phing) hot and crispy.
    - They can be enjoyed on their own or with a dipping sauce such as sweet chili sauce or a tangy dipping sauce made with lime juice, fish sauce, sugar, and chili.

Notes:

- **Variations:** Some recipes may include additional ingredients like chopped peanuts or water chestnuts for added texture.
- **Storage:** Leftover fried dumplings can be stored in an airtight container in the refrigerator for a few days. Reheat in the oven or toaster oven to crisp them up again.
- **Preparation Tip:** Make sure the filling is completely cooled before assembling the dumplings to prevent the wrappers from becoming soggy.

Enjoy your homemade Thai Fried Taro Dumplings (Khanom Phing) as a tasty and crispy snack or appetizer!

Thai Coconut Pancakes with Corn (Khanom Khrok Khao Pod)

Ingredients:

- 1 cup rice flour
- 1 cup coconut milk
- 1/2 cup sweet corn kernels (fresh or canned, drained)
- 1/4 cup sugar
- 1/4 teaspoon salt
- Vegetable oil or coconut oil, for cooking

Instructions:

1. **Prepare the Batter:**
   - In a mixing bowl, combine the rice flour, coconut milk, sugar, and salt. Mix well until smooth and no lumps remain.
2. **Add Sweet Corn:**
   - Stir in the sweet corn kernels into the batter, ensuring they are evenly distributed.
3. **Heat the Khanom Khrok Pan:**
   - Khanom Khrok pans are traditional Thai cookware used for making these pancakes. If you don't have one, you can use a small round pancake pan or an Æbleskiver pan (Danish pancake balls pan).
   - Heat the pan over medium heat and lightly grease the indentations with vegetable oil or coconut oil.
4. **Cook the Pancakes:**
   - Once the pan is hot, pour the batter into each indentation, filling them about 3/4 full.
   - Cover the pan with a lid and cook for about 3-4 minutes, or until the pancakes are set and golden brown on the bottom.
5. **Flip and Cook:**
   - Carefully flip each pancake using a small spatula or wooden skewer to cook the other side.
   - Cover again and cook for another 2-3 minutes, or until both sides are golden brown and cooked through.
6. **Serve:**
   - Remove the pancakes from the pan and transfer them to a plate.
   - Repeat the cooking process with the remaining batter until all pancakes are cooked.
7. **Enjoy:**
   - Serve the Khanom Khrok Khao Pod warm as a snack or dessert.
   - They can be enjoyed on their own or with a drizzle of sweetened coconut milk on top.

Notes:

- **Variations:** You can add other ingredients such as chopped scallions, taro, or pumpkin to the batter for different flavors.
- **Storage:** Leftover pancakes can be stored in an airtight container in the refrigerator for up to 2 days. Reheat gently in a pan or microwave before serving.
- **Special Equipment:** If you don't have a Khanom Khrok pan, you can use a mini muffin tin as an alternative.

Enjoy making and savoring these delicious Thai Coconut Pancakes with Corn (Khanom Khrok Khao Pod) at home!

Thai Shrimp Congee (Jok Goong)

Ingredients:

- 1/2 cup jasmine rice
- 5 cups chicken broth (homemade or low sodium)
- 1 cup shrimp, peeled and deveined
- 2-3 cloves garlic, minced
- 1 tablespoon ginger, finely grated
- 2-3 green onions, thinly sliced
- 2 tablespoons fish sauce
- 1 tablespoon soy sauce
- 1 teaspoon sugar
- White pepper, to taste
- 1 tablespoon vegetable oil
- Optional garnishes: Fried garlic, sliced red chilies, cilantro leaves, lime wedges

Instructions:

1. **Rinse and Cook the Rice:**
    - Rinse the jasmine rice under cold water until the water runs clear.
    - In a pot, bring the chicken broth to a boil over medium-high heat.
    - Add the rinsed rice to the boiling broth, reduce heat to low, cover, and simmer for about 20-25 minutes, stirring occasionally, until the rice is soft and porridge-like in consistency.
2. **Prepare the Shrimp:**
    - While the rice is cooking, heat the vegetable oil in a separate pan over medium heat.
    - Add the minced garlic and grated ginger, and sauté for about 1-2 minutes until fragrant.
    - Add the shrimp to the pan and cook for 2-3 minutes until they turn pink and opaque. Remove from heat and set aside.
3. **Season the Congee:**
    - Once the rice is cooked to a porridge consistency, add the cooked shrimp along with any juices from the pan into the pot.
    - Stir in fish sauce, soy sauce, sugar, and white pepper. Adjust seasoning to taste.
4. **Simmer and Serve:**
    - Let the congee simmer for another 5-10 minutes to allow the flavors to meld together.
    - Stir in thinly sliced green onions.
    - Ladle the shrimp congee into serving bowls.
5. **Garnish and Serve:**
    - Garnish each bowl with fried garlic, sliced red chilies, and cilantro leaves, if desired.

- Serve hot with lime wedges on the side for squeezing over the congee.

Notes:

- **Variations:** You can add other ingredients like sliced mushrooms, shredded chicken, or century eggs for additional flavor and texture.
- **Storage:** Leftover congee can be stored in an airtight container in the refrigerator for up to 3 days. Reheat gently on the stove or in the microwave, adding a splash of water or broth to adjust the consistency.
- **Texture:** Adjust the thickness of the congee by adding more broth or water if desired, especially when reheating.

Enjoy your homemade Thai Shrimp Congee (Jok Goong) for a comforting and satisfying meal!

Thai Spicy Beef Salad (Yam Nua)

Ingredients:

For the Beef:

- 1 lb beef sirloin or flank steak, thinly sliced
- 2 cloves garlic, minced
- 1 tablespoon soy sauce
- 1 tablespoon fish sauce
- 1 tablespoon oyster sauce
- 1 tablespoon vegetable oil
- Salt and pepper, to taste

For the Salad:

- 1 small red onion, thinly sliced
- 1-2 tomatoes, cut into wedges or slices
- 1 cucumber, thinly sliced
- 1 cup mixed greens (optional)
- Handful of fresh cilantro leaves, chopped
- Handful of fresh mint leaves, chopped
- Handful of fresh Thai basil leaves, chopped (optional)

For the Dressing:

- 3 tablespoons lime juice (about 2 limes)
- 2 tablespoons fish sauce
- 1 tablespoon soy sauce
- 1 tablespoon palm sugar or brown sugar
- 1-2 Thai bird's eye chilies, thinly sliced (adjust to taste)
- 2 cloves garlic, minced

Optional Garnishes:

- Roasted peanuts, chopped
- Fried shallots
- Sliced red chili peppers

Instructions:

1. **Marinate and Cook the Beef:**
   - In a bowl, combine the thinly sliced beef with minced garlic, soy sauce, fish sauce, oyster sauce, vegetable oil, salt, and pepper. Mix well to coat the beef evenly.

- Let the beef marinate for at least 15-30 minutes.
2. **Grill the Beef:**
   - Heat a grill or grill pan over medium-high heat.
   - Grill the marinated beef slices for 2-3 minutes per side, or until cooked to your desired doneness (medium-rare to medium is typical). Remove from heat and let it rest for a few minutes.
3. **Prepare the Dressing:**
   - In a small bowl, whisk together lime juice, fish sauce, soy sauce, palm sugar, Thai bird's eye chilies, and minced garlic until the sugar is dissolved.
4. **Assemble the Salad:**
   - In a large bowl, combine the sliced red onion, tomatoes, cucumber, mixed greens (if using), chopped cilantro, mint, and Thai basil leaves.
5. **Slice and Add the Beef:**
   - Slice the grilled beef thinly against the grain.
   - Add the sliced beef to the bowl of vegetables and herbs.
6. **Toss with Dressing:**
   - Pour the dressing over the salad ingredients.
   - Toss everything together gently until well combined and evenly coated with the dressing.
7. **Serve:**
   - Transfer the Thai Spicy Beef Salad (Yam Nua) to a serving platter or individual plates.
   - Garnish with chopped roasted peanuts, fried shallots, and sliced red chili peppers, if desired.
   - Serve immediately and enjoy the fresh, tangy flavors!

Notes:

- **Spice Level:** Adjust the amount of Thai bird's eye chilies to suit your preference for spiciness.
- **Variations:** Feel free to add other vegetables like bell peppers or bean sprouts to the salad for extra crunch and flavor.
- **Make Ahead:** You can marinate the beef and prepare the dressing ahead of time. Assemble the salad just before serving to keep the vegetables crisp.

Enjoy making and savoring this delicious Thai Spicy Beef Salad (Yam Nua) at home!

Thai Stir-Fried Glass Noodles (Pad Woon Sen)

Ingredients:

- 100g dried glass noodles (bean thread noodles)
- 150g shrimp, peeled and deveined (or chicken breast, thinly sliced)
- 2-3 cloves garlic, minced
- 1 small onion, thinly sliced
- 1 carrot, julienned
- 1 bell pepper, thinly sliced
- 1 cup cabbage, shredded
- 2-3 spring onions, cut into 2-inch pieces
- 2-3 tablespoons vegetable oil
- 2 tablespoons soy sauce
- 1 tablespoon oyster sauce
- 1 tablespoon fish sauce
- 1 tablespoon sugar
- 1/2 teaspoon ground white pepper
- Optional: Thai bird's eye chilies, thinly sliced (for spice)
- Fresh cilantro leaves, chopped (for garnish)
- Lime wedges (for serving)

Instructions:

1. **Prepare the Glass Noodles:**
    - Place the dried glass noodles in a large bowl and cover with hot water. Let them soak for about 10-15 minutes until they are soft and pliable. Drain and set aside.
2. **Prepare the Protein and Vegetables:**
    - If using shrimp, season them with a bit of salt and pepper. If using chicken, season with salt and pepper as well.
    - Heat 1 tablespoon of vegetable oil in a wok or large skillet over medium-high heat. Add the shrimp or chicken and cook until they are just cooked through. Remove from the wok and set aside.
3. **Stir-Fry the Vegetables:**
    - In the same wok or skillet, heat the remaining vegetable oil over medium-high heat.
    - Add minced garlic and stir-fry for about 30 seconds until fragrant.
    - Add the sliced onion, julienned carrot, and bell pepper. Stir-fry for 2-3 minutes until the vegetables start to soften.
4. **Add Cabbage and Noodles:**
    - Add the shredded cabbage to the wok and stir-fry for another 1-2 minutes until the cabbage begins to wilt.

- Add the soaked glass noodles to the wok, along with soy sauce, oyster sauce, fish sauce, sugar, and ground white pepper. Toss everything together gently to combine.

5. **Combine Everything:**
    - Return the cooked shrimp or chicken to the wok. Stir-fry for another 1-2 minutes until everything is heated through and well combined.
    - Taste and adjust seasoning if needed. If you like it spicy, add some thinly sliced Thai bird's eye chilies at this stage.
6. **Serve:**
    - Transfer the Pad Woon Sen to a serving platter or individual plates.
    - Garnish with chopped cilantro leaves.
    - Serve hot with lime wedges on the side for squeezing over the noodles.

Notes:

- **Vegetarian Option:** Omit the shrimp or chicken and use tofu or more vegetables for a vegetarian version.
- **Variations:** You can customize this dish with other vegetables such as mushrooms, snow peas, or baby corn.
- **Storage:** Leftovers can be stored in an airtight container in the refrigerator for up to 2 days. Reheat gently in a skillet or microwave before serving.

Enjoy your homemade Thai Stir-Fried Glass Noodles (Pad Woon Sen) as a delicious and satisfying meal!

Thai Pork and Rice Congee (Khao Tom Moo)

Ingredients:

- 1 cup jasmine rice
- 6 cups chicken broth (homemade or low sodium)
- 250g ground pork
- 3-4 cloves garlic, minced
- 1 tablespoon ginger, finely grated
- 2-3 green onions, thinly sliced
- 1 tablespoon soy sauce
- 1 tablespoon fish sauce
- 1 teaspoon sugar
- White pepper, to taste
- Vegetable oil, for cooking
- Optional garnishes: Fried garlic, sliced red chilies, cilantro leaves, lime wedges

Instructions:

1. **Prepare the Rice:**
   - Rinse the jasmine rice under cold water until the water runs clear.
   - In a large pot, bring the chicken broth to a boil over medium-high heat.
   - Add the rinsed rice to the boiling broth, reduce heat to low, cover, and simmer for about 20-25 minutes, stirring occasionally, until the rice is soft and broken down into a porridge-like consistency.
2. **Cook the Pork:**
   - While the rice is cooking, heat a bit of vegetable oil in a separate pan over medium heat.
   - Add minced garlic and grated ginger, and sauté for about 1-2 minutes until fragrant.
   - Add the ground pork to the pan and cook, breaking it up with a spatula, until browned and cooked through.
3. **Season the Congee:**
   - Add the cooked ground pork to the pot of rice porridge.
   - Stir in soy sauce, fish sauce, sugar, and white pepper. Adjust seasoning to taste.
4. **Simmer and Serve:**
   - Let the Khao Tom Moo simmer for another 5-10 minutes to allow the flavors to meld together.
   - Stir in thinly sliced green onions.
5. **Garnish and Serve:**
   - Ladle the pork and rice congee into serving bowls.
   - Garnish with fried garlic, sliced red chilies, and cilantro leaves, if desired.
   - Serve hot with lime wedges on the side for squeezing over the congee.

Notes:

- **Texture Adjustment:** If the congee becomes too thick upon standing, you can stir in additional hot water or broth to achieve your desired consistency.
- **Variations:** You can add additional ingredients such as chopped century eggs, sliced mushrooms, or even a beaten egg stirred in for extra richness.
- **Storage:** Leftover congee can be stored in an airtight container in the refrigerator for up to 3 days. Reheat gently on the stove or in the microwave, adding a splash of water or broth to adjust the consistency.

Enjoy your homemade Thai Pork and Rice Congee (Khao Tom Moo) for a comforting and satisfying meal!

Thai Coconut Milk Custard (Sangkhaya)

Ingredients:

- 4 eggs
- 1 cup coconut milk
- 1/2 cup palm sugar (or brown sugar)
- 1/4 teaspoon salt
- Banana leaves or foil, for wrapping (optional)

Instructions:

1. **Prepare the Custard Mixture:**
   - In a mixing bowl, whisk together the eggs, coconut milk, palm sugar, and salt until well combined and the sugar is dissolved. Strain the mixture through a fine sieve to ensure a smooth texture.
2. **Cooking Method:**
   - Traditional Method (Steaming):
     - Prepare a steamer by bringing water to a boil.
     - If using banana leaves, briefly pass them over an open flame to soften them. Line small bowls or ramekins with banana leaves or lightly greased foil.
     - Pour the custard mixture into the prepared bowls or ramekins.
     - Place the bowls or ramekins in the steamer, cover with a lid, and steam over medium heat for about 20-25 minutes, or until the custard is set. To check for doneness, insert a toothpick into the center of the custard; it should come out clean.
   - Oven Method:
     - Preheat your oven to 350°F (175°C).
     - Place the filled ramekins or bowls in a baking dish. Fill the baking dish with hot water halfway up the sides of the ramekins.
     - Bake in the preheated oven for about 30-40 minutes, or until the custard is set and slightly golden on top.
3. **Serve:**
   - Once the custard is cooked and set, remove from heat.
   - Let the custards cool to room temperature before serving.
   - Optionally, garnish with a sprinkle of shredded coconut or a drizzle of coconut milk on top.
4. **Storage:**
   - Store any leftover custard in the refrigerator. It can be enjoyed chilled or brought back to room temperature before serving.

Notes:

- **Variations:** You can enhance the flavor of Sangkhaya by adding pandan extract for a fragrant twist, or by sprinkling toasted sesame seeds on top before serving.
- **Presentation:** Traditionally, Sangkhaya is often served in small individual bowls or ramekins, sometimes lined with banana leaves for an added aroma.
- **Texture:** The texture should be smooth and slightly firm, similar to a flan or crème caramel.

Enjoy your homemade Thai Coconut Milk Custard (Sangkhaya) as a delightful and authentic Thai dessert!

Thai Peanut Pancakes (Khanom Thua Paep)

Ingredients:

- 4 eggs
- 1 cup coconut milk
- 1/2 cup palm sugar (or brown sugar)
- 1/4 teaspoon salt
- Banana leaves or foil, for wrapping (optional)

Instructions:

1. **Prepare the Custard Mixture:**
   - In a mixing bowl, whisk together the eggs, coconut milk, palm sugar, and salt until well combined and the sugar is dissolved. Strain the mixture through a fine sieve to ensure a smooth texture.
2. **Cooking Method:**
   - Traditional Method (Steaming):
     - Prepare a steamer by bringing water to a boil.
     - If using banana leaves, briefly pass them over an open flame to soften them. Line small bowls or ramekins with banana leaves or lightly greased foil.
     - Pour the custard mixture into the prepared bowls or ramekins.
     - Place the bowls or ramekins in the steamer, cover with a lid, and steam over medium heat for about 20-25 minutes, or until the custard is set. To check for doneness, insert a toothpick into the center of the custard; it should come out clean.
   - Oven Method:
     - Preheat your oven to 350°F (175°C).
     - Place the filled ramekins or bowls in a baking dish. Fill the baking dish with hot water halfway up the sides of the ramekins.
     - Bake in the preheated oven for about 30-40 minutes, or until the custard is set and slightly golden on top.
3. **Serve:**
   - Once the custard is cooked and set, remove from heat.
   - Let the custards cool to room temperature before serving.
   - Optionally, garnish with a sprinkle of shredded coconut or a drizzle of coconut milk on top.
4. **Storage:**
   - Store any leftover custard in the refrigerator. It can be enjoyed chilled or brought back to room temperature before serving.

Notes:

- **Variations:** You can enhance the flavor of Sangkhaya by adding pandan extract for a fragrant twist, or by sprinkling toasted sesame seeds on top before serving.
- **Presentation:** Traditionally, Sangkhaya is often served in small individual bowls or ramekins, sometimes lined with banana leaves for an added aroma.
- **Texture:** The texture should be smooth and slightly firm, similar to a flan or crème caramel.

Enjoy your homemade Thai Coconut Milk Custard (Sangkhaya) as a delightful and authentic Thai dessert!

Thai Spicy Squid Salad (Yam Pla Muk)

Ingredients:

- 300g squid tubes, cleaned and sliced into rings
- 1 cup cherry tomatoes, halved
- 1/2 cup red onion, thinly sliced
- 1/2 cup cucumber, thinly sliced
- 1/4 cup cilantro (coriander) leaves, chopped
- 1/4 cup mint leaves, chopped
- 2-3 spring onions, thinly sliced
- 2-3 Thai bird's eye chilies, thinly sliced (adjust to taste)
- 2 tablespoons roasted peanuts, chopped (optional, for garnish)

For the Dressing:

- 3 tablespoons lime juice (about 2 limes)
- 2 tablespoons fish sauce
- 1 tablespoon soy sauce
- 1 tablespoon palm sugar (or brown sugar)
- 1-2 cloves garlic, minced
- 1 teaspoon dried chili flakes (adjust to taste)

Instructions:

1. **Prepare the Squid:**
   - If using fresh squid, clean them thoroughly and slice into rings. If using frozen squid, thaw according to package instructions.
2. **Blanch the Squid:**
   - Bring a pot of water to a boil. Add the squid rings and blanch for about 1-2 minutes until they turn opaque and curl up. Be careful not to overcook. Drain and set aside.
3. **Prepare the Dressing:**
   - In a small bowl, whisk together lime juice, fish sauce, soy sauce, palm sugar, minced garlic, and dried chili flakes until the sugar is dissolved.
4. **Assemble the Salad:**
   - In a large mixing bowl, combine the blanched squid rings, cherry tomatoes, red onion, cucumber, chopped cilantro, mint leaves, spring onions, and sliced Thai bird's eye chilies.
5. **Add the Dressing:**
   - Pour the dressing over the salad ingredients. Toss gently to combine, ensuring everything is coated evenly with the dressing.
6. **Garnish and Serve:**
   - Transfer the Yam Pla Muk to a serving platter or individual plates.
   - Garnish with chopped roasted peanuts, if using.

- Serve immediately and enjoy the vibrant flavors of this Thai Spicy Squid Salad!

Notes:

- **Adjust Spice Level:** You can adjust the amount of Thai bird's eye chilies and dried chili flakes according to your preference for spiciness.
- **Make Ahead:** You can prepare the dressing and blanch the squid ahead of time. Assemble the salad just before serving to keep the ingredients fresh.
- **Variations:** Feel free to add other vegetables such as bell peppers, lettuce, or bean sprouts for extra texture and flavor.

Enjoy making and savoring this delicious Thai Spicy Squid Salad (Yam Pla Muk) as a refreshing appetizer or light meal!

Thai Stir-Fried Pork with Basil (Pad Kra Pao Moo)

Ingredients:

- 300g ground pork (or thinly sliced pork loin)
- 3-4 cloves garlic, minced
- 2-3 Thai bird's eye chilies, finely chopped (adjust to taste)
- 1 cup fresh basil leaves (Thai basil if available)
- 1 tablespoon vegetable oil
- 1 tablespoon oyster sauce
- 1 tablespoon soy sauce
- 1 teaspoon fish sauce
- 1 teaspoon sugar
- 1/4 cup chicken broth or water
- Jasmine rice and fried egg, for serving

Instructions:

1. **Prepare the Ingredients:**
    - Heat vegetable oil in a wok or large skillet over medium-high heat.
2. **Cook the Pork:**
    - Add minced garlic and chopped Thai bird's eye chilies to the heated oil. Stir-fry for about 30 seconds until fragrant.
    - Add ground pork (or thinly sliced pork) to the wok. Break up the pork with a spatula and stir-fry until it is cooked through and no longer pink.
3. **Season the Dish:**
    - Stir in oyster sauce, soy sauce, fish sauce, and sugar. Mix well to combine with the pork.
4. **Add Basil Leaves:**
    - Add fresh basil leaves to the wok. Stir-fry for another minute until the basil leaves are wilted and aromatic.
5. **Moisten with Broth or Water:**
    - Pour chicken broth or water into the wok to create a bit of sauce. Stir well to incorporate all the flavors.
6. **Serve:**
    - Serve Pad Kra Pao Moo hot with jasmine rice and a fried egg on top.
    - Optionally, garnish with additional fresh basil leaves or sliced Thai bird's eye chilies for extra spice.

Notes:

- **Variations:** You can substitute pork with chicken, beef, or even tofu for a different protein option.

- **Spice Level:** Adjust the amount of Thai bird's eye chilies according to your preference for spiciness.
- **Egg Preparation:** For a traditional serving, fry an egg sunny-side-up or over-easy and place it on top of the rice next to the stir-fried pork.

Enjoy your homemade Thai Stir-Fried Pork with Basil (Pad Kra Pao Moo) for a delicious and satisfying meal packed with Thai flavors!

Thai Coconut Ice Cream (I-Tim Kati)

Ingredients:

- 2 cups coconut milk
- 1 cup heavy cream
- 3/4 cup sugar
- 1/4 teaspoon salt
- 1 teaspoon vanilla extract (optional)
- Toppings (optional): Roasted peanuts, sweet sticky rice, coconut flakes, condensed milk

Instructions:

1. **Mix the Ingredients:**
   - In a saucepan, combine coconut milk, heavy cream, sugar, and salt over medium heat.
   - Stir continuously until the mixture is smooth and the sugar has completely dissolved. Do not let it boil.
2. **Cool the Mixture:**
   - Remove the saucepan from heat and let the mixture cool to room temperature.
   - Optionally, stir in vanilla extract for additional flavor.
3. **Chill the Mixture:**
   - Once cooled, transfer the mixture to a container and refrigerate for at least 2 hours, or until thoroughly chilled. Chilling overnight is ideal for best results.
4. **Churn the Ice Cream:**
   - Pour the chilled mixture into an ice cream maker and churn according to the manufacturer's instructions until it reaches a soft-serve consistency.
5. **Freeze the Ice Cream:**
   - Transfer the churned ice cream into a freezer-safe container.
   - Cover with plastic wrap or a lid and freeze for at least 4 hours, or until firm.
6. **Serve:**
   - Scoop the Thai Coconut Ice Cream into bowls or cones.
   - Serve with toppings such as roasted peanuts, sweet sticky rice, coconut flakes, or a drizzle of condensed milk, if desired.

Notes:

- **Coconut Milk:** Use full-fat coconut milk for a richer and creamier texture.
- **Heavy Cream:** Helps add creaminess to the ice cream.
- **Sugar:** Adjust the amount of sugar according to your sweetness preference.
- **Storage:** Store leftover ice cream in an airtight container in the freezer for up to 2 weeks.

Enjoy your homemade Thai Coconut Ice Cream (I-Tim Kati) as a delightful treat that captures the tropical flavors of Thailand!

Thai Fish Cakes (Tod Mun Pla)

Ingredients:

- 300g firm white fish fillets (such as cod or tilapia), deboned and roughly chopped
- 1 tablespoon red curry paste
- 1 egg
- 2 tablespoons fish sauce
- 1 tablespoon palm sugar or brown sugar
- 1 tablespoon lime juice
- 1 kaffir lime leaf, finely shredded (optional)
- 1/4 cup green beans, finely chopped
- 1/4 cup fresh cilantro (coriander) leaves and stems, finely chopped
- Vegetable oil, for frying

Dipping Sauce:

- 1/4 cup cucumber, finely diced
- 1/4 cup shallots, finely sliced
- 1/4 cup roasted peanuts, coarsely ground
- 1 tablespoon sugar
- 1 tablespoon vinegar
- 1 tablespoon fish sauce
- 1 tablespoon water
- 1-2 Thai bird's eye chilies, finely chopped (optional)

Instructions:

1. **Prepare the Dipping Sauce:**
    - In a small bowl, combine cucumber, shallots, roasted peanuts, sugar, vinegar, fish sauce, water, and Thai bird's eye chilies (if using). Mix well and set aside.
2. **Make the Fish Cake Mixture:**
    - In a food processor, blend the chopped fish fillets until smooth.
    - Add red curry paste, egg, fish sauce, palm sugar, lime juice, and shredded kaffir lime leaf (if using). Blend until well combined.
3. **Add Vegetables and Herbs:**
    - Transfer the fish mixture to a bowl.
    - Fold in chopped green beans and cilantro until evenly distributed in the mixture.
4. **Form and Fry the Fish Cakes:**
    - Heat vegetable oil in a frying pan or wok over medium-high heat.
    - Take about 1 tablespoon of the fish mixture and shape it into a small patty using wet hands to prevent sticking.
    - Carefully place the fish cakes into the hot oil and fry for about 3-4 minutes on each side, or until golden brown and cooked through.
    - Fry in batches to avoid overcrowding the pan.
5. **Serve:**

- Drain the fish cakes on paper towels to remove excess oil.
- Serve hot with the prepared dipping sauce on the side.

Notes:

- **Variations:** You can substitute the fish with shrimp or a combination of seafood for different flavors.
- **Make Ahead:** The fish cake mixture can be prepared in advance and refrigerated. Fry them just before serving for the best texture.
- **Crispiness:** For extra crispiness, you can lightly dust the fish cakes with rice flour or cornstarch before frying.

Enjoy your homemade Thai Fish Cakes (Tod Mun Pla) with the flavorful dipping sauce for an authentic taste of Thailand!

Thai Deep Fried Bananas (Kluay Tod)

Ingredients:

- 4 ripe bananas (such as Thai bananas or ladyfinger bananas)
- 1 cup all-purpose flour
- 1/4 cup rice flour (optional, for extra crispiness)
- 1/4 cup desiccated coconut (optional, for added texture)
- 1/4 cup sugar
- 1/2 teaspoon baking powder
- 1/4 teaspoon salt
- 1 cup water or coconut milk (adjust consistency as needed)
- Vegetable oil, for frying
- Honey or powdered sugar, for dusting (optional)

Instructions:

1. **Prepare the Bananas:**
   - Peel the bananas and cut them into halves or thirds, depending on their size. You can also cut them into smaller pieces if desired.
2. **Prepare the Batter:**
   - In a mixing bowl, combine all-purpose flour, rice flour (if using), desiccated coconut (if using), sugar, baking powder, and salt.
   - Gradually add water or coconut milk, whisking continuously, until you achieve a smooth and thick batter that coats the back of a spoon. The consistency should be similar to pancake batter.
3. **Heat the Oil:**
   - Heat vegetable oil in a deep frying pan or pot over medium-high heat. The oil should be hot enough for frying (around 350°F or 180°C).
4. **Coat and Fry the Bananas:**
   - Dip each banana piece into the batter, ensuring it is evenly coated.
   - Carefully place the coated banana pieces into the hot oil, a few at a time, depending on the size of your frying vessel. Avoid overcrowding.
5. **Fry Until Golden Brown:**
   - Fry the bananas for about 2-3 minutes on each side, or until they are golden brown and crispy.
6. **Drain and Serve:**
   - Remove the fried bananas from the oil using a slotted spoon and drain on paper towels to remove excess oil.
7. **Serve Warm:**
   - Serve the Thai Deep Fried Bananas (Kluay Tod) warm.
   - Optionally, drizzle with honey or dust with powdered sugar before serving for extra sweetness.

Notes:

- **Banana Varieties:** Thai bananas (also known as ladyfinger bananas or finger bananas) are preferred for this dish due to their sweetness and texture, but you can use regular bananas if Thai bananas are not available.
- **Texture Variations:** Adding desiccated coconut to the batter adds texture and enhances the flavor, but it's optional.
- **Storage:** These are best enjoyed fresh and warm. Leftovers can be stored in an airtight container in the refrigerator and reheated in the oven to regain crispiness.

Enjoy your homemade Thai Deep Fried Bananas (Kluay Tod) as a delightful snack or dessert with a cup of tea or coffee!

Thai Chicken Curry with Bamboo Shoots (Gang Kiew Wan Gai)

Ingredients:

- 500g chicken thighs or breast, cut into bite-sized pieces
- 2-3 tablespoons green curry paste (store-bought or homemade)
- 1 can (400ml) coconut milk
- 1 cup bamboo shoots, sliced (fresh or canned, drained)
- 1 red bell pepper, sliced
- 1 small eggplant, cut into chunks
- 1-2 tablespoons fish sauce, to taste
- 1 tablespoon palm sugar or brown sugar, to taste
- 1 cup Thai basil leaves (or regular basil leaves)
- Vegetable oil
- Fresh red chili slices, for garnish (optional)
- Cooked jasmine rice, for serving

Green Curry Paste (Homemade, optional):

- 2-3 fresh green Thai chilies, chopped (adjust to taste)
- 2 stalks lemongrass, sliced (white part only)
- 4-5 cloves garlic
- 1 shallot, chopped
- 1 thumb-sized piece of galangal or ginger, sliced
- 1 teaspoon ground coriander
- 1/2 teaspoon ground cumin
- 1/2 teaspoon shrimp paste (optional)
- Zest of 1 lime (optional)

Instructions:

1. **Prepare the Green Curry Paste (if making from scratch):**
   - In a mortar and pestle or a food processor, pound or blend together all the green curry paste ingredients until a smooth paste forms. Add a little water if needed to help blend.
2. **Cook the Chicken:**
   - Heat a tablespoon of vegetable oil in a large skillet or wok over medium heat.
   - Add the green curry paste and stir-fry for 1-2 minutes until fragrant.
3. **Add Coconut Milk:**
   - Pour in about half of the coconut milk (200ml) into the skillet. Stir and cook for another 1-2 minutes until the coconut milk is heated through and slightly thickened.
4. **Add Chicken:**
   - Add the chicken pieces to the skillet and stir to coat them with the curry paste and coconut milk mixture.
5. **Simmer:**

- Let the chicken simmer in the curry mixture for about 5-7 minutes, or until the chicken is cooked through and tender.
6. **Add Vegetables:**
   - Add bamboo shoots, sliced red bell pepper, and eggplant chunks to the skillet. Stir to combine.
7. **Season:**
   - Season with fish sauce and palm sugar (or brown sugar) to taste. Adjust the seasoning according to your preference for saltiness and sweetness.
8. **Simmer Further:**
   - Allow the curry to simmer gently for another 5-10 minutes, or until the vegetables are cooked to your liking and the flavors have melded together.
9. **Add Thai Basil:**
   - Stir in Thai basil leaves (or regular basil leaves) just before serving. The heat from the curry will wilt the basil slightly.
10. **Serve:**
    - Serve the Thai Chicken Curry with Bamboo Shoots (Gang Kiew Wan Gai) hot, garnished with fresh red chili slices (if using), alongside jasmine rice.

Notes:

- **Green Curry Paste:** While store-bought curry paste is convenient, making it from scratch allows you to adjust the spiciness and flavors to your liking.
- **Vegetables:** Feel free to add other vegetables such as Thai eggplants, snow peas, or baby corn.
- **Storage:** Leftover curry can be stored in an airtight container in the refrigerator for up to 3 days. Reheat gently on the stove or in the microwave before serving.

Enjoy making and savoring this delicious Thai Chicken Curry with Bamboo Shoots (Gang Kiew Wan Gai) at home!

Thai Spicy Noodle Soup (Tom Yum Goong)

Ingredients:

- 4 cups chicken or seafood broth
- 200g shrimp, peeled and deveined (you can also use other seafood like squid or fish fillets)
- 3-4 kaffir lime leaves, torn or sliced thinly
- 1 stalk lemongrass, cut into 2-inch pieces and bruised
- 3-4 slices galangal or ginger
- 4-6 Thai bird's eye chilies, crushed (adjust to taste)
- 3-4 cloves garlic, smashed
- 1-2 tomatoes, cut into wedges
- 1 small onion, thinly sliced
- 1 cup mushrooms (straw mushrooms or button mushrooms), sliced
- 2 tablespoons fish sauce
- 1-2 tablespoons lime juice
- 1 tablespoon palm sugar or brown sugar (optional)
- 1/4 cup fresh cilantro (coriander) leaves, chopped
- 1/4 cup fresh Thai basil leaves (optional)
- Salt, to taste

Instructions:

1. **Prepare the Broth:**
   - In a pot, bring the chicken or seafood broth to a boil over medium-high heat.
2. **Add Aromatics:**
   - Add kaffir lime leaves, lemongrass, galangal or ginger, crushed Thai chilies, and smashed garlic cloves to the boiling broth. Simmer for about 5-10 minutes to infuse the broth with flavors.
3. **Add Vegetables:**
   - Add tomatoes, onion slices, and mushrooms to the broth. Cook for another 3-5 minutes until the vegetables are slightly tender.
4. **Season the Soup:**
   - Stir in fish sauce, lime juice, and palm sugar (if using). Adjust the seasoning to achieve a balance of salty, sour, and spicy flavors.
5. **Add Shrimp (or other seafood):**
   - Add shrimp (or other seafood like squid or fish) to the pot. Cook for 2-3 minutes or until the shrimp are pink and cooked through.
6. **Finish with Herbs:**
   - Remove the pot from heat. Stir in chopped cilantro and Thai basil leaves (if using). These fresh herbs will add brightness and aroma to the soup.
7. **Serve:**
   - Ladle the Tom Yum Goong into serving bowls.
   - Garnish with additional fresh cilantro leaves and Thai bird's eye chilies if desired.
   - Serve hot as a soup course or with steamed jasmine rice.

Notes:

- **Variations:** You can adjust the ingredients based on your preference. For a vegetarian version, omit the shrimp and use vegetable broth or add tofu instead.
- **Spice Level:** Adjust the amount of Thai bird's eye chilies according to your preference for spiciness.
- **Storage:** Tom Yum Goong is best enjoyed fresh. Leftovers can be stored in an airtight container in the refrigerator for up to 2 days. Reheat gently on the stove before serving.

Enjoy your homemade Tom Yum Goong, a delightful and comforting Thai spicy noodle soup!

Thai Fried Rice with Shrimp (Khao Pad Goong)

Ingredients:

- 2 cups cooked jasmine rice (preferably cooled or day-old)
- 200g shrimp, peeled and deveined
- 2 eggs, beaten
- 1 cup mixed vegetables (such as peas, carrots, and bell peppers), diced
- 3 cloves garlic, minced
- 1 small onion, diced
- 2-3 Thai bird's eye chilies, finely chopped (adjust to taste)
- 2 tablespoons vegetable oil
- 2 tablespoons fish sauce
- 1 tablespoon soy sauce
- 1 tablespoon oyster sauce
- 1 teaspoon sugar
- Fresh cilantro (coriander) leaves for garnish
- Lime wedges for serving

Instructions:

1. **Prepare Ingredients:**
   - If using freshly cooked rice, spread it out on a tray to cool completely. Day-old rice works best for fried rice as it is drier and less sticky.
2. **Cook the Shrimp:**
   - Heat 1 tablespoon of vegetable oil in a large wok or skillet over medium-high heat.
   - Add shrimp and stir-fry for 2-3 minutes until pink and cooked through. Remove shrimp from the wok and set aside.
3. **Scramble Eggs:**
   - In the same wok or skillet, add another tablespoon of vegetable oil.
   - Pour in the beaten eggs and scramble until fully cooked. Remove scrambled eggs from the wok and set aside with the cooked shrimp.
4. **Stir-fry Vegetables:**
   - Add minced garlic, diced onion, and Thai bird's eye chilies to the wok. Stir-fry for 1-2 minutes until fragrant.
5. **Combine Rice and Sauce:**
   - Add the cooked jasmine rice to the wok. Use a spatula to break up any clumps of rice and stir-fry with the vegetables.
6. **Add Sauces:**
   - Drizzle fish sauce, soy sauce, oyster sauce, and sugar over the rice. Stir-fry for another 2-3 minutes to ensure the rice is well coated with the sauce.
7. **Combine Everything:**
   - Return the cooked shrimp and scrambled eggs to the wok. Add diced mixed vegetables. Stir-fry everything together for another 2-3 minutes until heated through.

8. **Finish and Serve:**
    - Taste and adjust seasoning if needed with more fish sauce, soy sauce, or sugar.
    - Garnish with fresh cilantro leaves and serve hot.
    - Serve Khao Pad Goong with lime wedges on the side for squeezing over the rice before eating.

Notes:

- **Variations:** You can customize Khao Pad Goong by adding other ingredients such as pineapple chunks, cashew nuts, or basil leaves for different flavors and textures.
- **Rice:** Using day-old rice helps prevent it from becoming mushy during stir-frying.
- **Spice Level:** Adjust the amount of Thai bird's eye chilies according to your preference for spiciness.
- **Storage:** Leftover fried rice can be stored in an airtight container in the refrigerator for up to 2 days. Reheat gently in a wok or microwave before serving.

Enjoy your homemade Thai Fried Rice with Shrimp (Khao Pad Goong) as a delicious and satisfying meal!

Thai Grilled Pork Neck Salad (Yam Kor Moo Yang)

Ingredients:

For the Grilled Pork Neck:

- 500g pork neck or pork shoulder, thinly sliced
- 2 tablespoons soy sauce
- 2 tablespoons oyster sauce
- 1 tablespoon fish sauce
- 1 tablespoon sugar
- 1 teaspoon ground white pepper
- 3 cloves garlic, minced
- 1 tablespoon vegetable oil

For the Salad:

- 1 small red onion, thinly sliced
- 1/2 cup cherry tomatoes, halved
- 1 cucumber, thinly sliced
- 1/2 cup fresh cilantro (coriander) leaves, chopped
- 1/4 cup fresh mint leaves, chopped
- 1-2 Thai bird's eye chilies, thinly sliced (adjust to taste)

For the Dressing:

- 3 tablespoons lime juice
- 2 tablespoons fish sauce
- 1 tablespoon palm sugar or brown sugar
- 1-2 cloves garlic, minced
- 1-2 Thai bird's eye chilies, finely chopped (adjust to taste)

Instructions:

1. **Marinate and Grill the Pork Neck:**
   - In a bowl, combine soy sauce, oyster sauce, fish sauce, sugar, ground white pepper, minced garlic, and vegetable oil. Mix well.
   - Add the thinly sliced pork neck to the marinade. Toss to coat evenly. Marinate for at least 30 minutes, or preferably overnight for best flavor.
   - Preheat a grill pan or barbecue grill over medium-high heat. Grill the marinated pork neck slices for 3-4 minutes on each side, or until fully cooked and charred with grill marks. Remove from heat and let it rest.
2. **Prepare the Salad:**
   - In a large mixing bowl, combine thinly sliced red onion, halved cherry tomatoes, thinly sliced cucumber, chopped fresh cilantro, chopped fresh mint leaves, and sliced Thai bird's eye chilies.
3. **Make the Dressing:**

- In a small bowl, whisk together lime juice, fish sauce, palm sugar (or brown sugar), minced garlic, and chopped Thai bird's eye chilies until the sugar is dissolved.
4. **Assemble the Salad:**
    - Add the grilled pork neck slices to the bowl of prepared salad ingredients.
    - Pour the dressing over the salad and grilled pork. Toss gently to combine, ensuring everything is coated with the dressing.
5. **Serve:**
    - Transfer the Yam Kor Moo Yang to a serving platter or individual plates.
    - Garnish with additional cilantro leaves and mint leaves if desired.
    - Serve immediately and enjoy the delicious flavors of Thai Grilled Pork Neck Salad!

Notes:

- **Variations:** You can adjust the spiciness by adding more or less Thai bird's eye chilies to both the salad and the dressing.
- **Grilling Alternatives:** If you don't have a grill, you can pan-fry the pork neck slices in a skillet over medium-high heat until cooked through.
- **Make Ahead:** The pork can be grilled ahead of time and refrigerated. Assemble the salad and toss with the dressing just before serving to maintain freshness.

Enjoy making and savoring this Thai Grilled Pork Neck Salad (Yam Kor Moo Yang) as a refreshing and flavorful dish!

www.ingramcontent.com/pod-product-compliance
Lightning Source LLC
LaVergne TN
LVHW081559060526
838201LV00054B/1964